∽ *My Soul on Paper II: Even Deeper*

My Soul on Paper II: Even Deeper

BY LAQUANIA SHEREE GRAHAM

Published by Asta Publications, LLC
P.O. Box 1735
Stockbridge, Georgia

Copyright © Laquania Graham, 2007
All rights reserved. Published 2007

No part of the contents of this book may be reproduced or transmitted in any form or by any means without the written permission of the publisher. Your support of the author's rights is appreciated.

Text and composition: Erin Kirk New

Library of Congress Cataloging in Publication Data

Graham, Laquania
p.
ISBN: 13 978-0-9777060-8-2
ISBN: 0-9777060-8-7
LCCN: 2007942610
First Asta Publications, LLC trade paperback edition December 2007
1. African American women-Poetry. 2. African American relationships-nonfiction. 3. Selfrealization-poetry. 4. Women-nonfiction. I. Title

*This book is dedicated to Mr. Alonza Price for holding on "just a little while longer."
I love you.*

Contents

Prayer
Introduction

PART I ~ DEEPER

Touch Me   3
My Greatest Enemy   9
Wanted   13
Bleeding   16
He Wins   20

PART II ~ TEA TIME

My Tribute   29
Skin Deep   31
Off By a Shade   35

PART III ~ A ROSE AMONG THORNS

Pray for the Prey   44
The Cost of the Anointing   46
The Kingdom Has Need of You   50
I Still Believe in Fairy Tales   56
Expensive   58

PART IV ~ HE DIDN'T DESERVE ME

Never Say Never   63
You Didn't Deserve Me   67
Midnight Girl   69
He Wants Me to Wait   73
The Tin Man   77
He Cut Me Loose   81

PART V ~ A DAY IN THE LIFE

In My Shoes   87
Polished   91
Face Value   93
Invasion   95
Wait Your Turn   98

PART VI ~ I LOVE ME SOME HIM

While He Slept   103
I Admire You   105
Naked and Not Ashamed   108

PART VII ~ SISTA TO SISTA

She Expects Me to Fail   117
What's Due   120
Power of the Body   122
Ammunition   127

Afterword   135
Acknowledgments   137
About the Author   141

Prayer

*For this cause I bow my knees unto the Father of
our Lord Jesus Christ.—Ephesians 3:14 KJV*

Lord, I thank you for the person who now holds my story in their hands. Thank you for giving them the opportunity to share my world. I thank you in advance for the wounds and scars you're getting ready to heal as a result of all the tears that were shed. I pray for this person's strength and ability to get past all that they have gone through up until this point. I know that there is nothing too hard for you and that you can encourage this person to forgive and move on. Convict their heart and wash them from the stains of life. Hide them from the snare of the enemy.

I ask that you prepare this individual for what lies ahead and propel them into their future. Help this person walk into the purpose and calling that you have destined for them long before they were even thought of. Allow this individual to put their Godgiven talents to use and to no longer voice meaningless excuses as to why their dreams are unattainable.

It was no accident or coincidence that this person has this book, whether they sowed into the ministry, picked it up at the library, or borrowed it from someone else. Give them the hope they're looking for.

These things I pray for in your son Jesus' name,

Amen.

Introduction

When my brother and I released *My Soul on Paper*, I had no idea that so many people would go to such extreme measures to obtain copies of the book in order to find out what family secrets we had possibly disclosed. It was silly of me to think that everyone would have good intentions when they were running to the bookstores to get their copy, but I did. I later found out that the paparazzi didn't have anything on my neighborhood!

What these people didn't know was that the poems I have written throughout my life have been a mixture of my own experiences, as well as the experiences of people I knew personally, heard on TV and even through various sermons. So in response to a number of questions about whether I was sexually assaulted by a boyfriend or husband of my mom's is a resounding "No."

In *My Soul on Paper II: Even Deeper*, I placed myself under the spotlight so that you can search for and identify yourself through my writings. I didn't dare waste space or energy by pointing out which poem or line is actually biographic. Just know that I experienced a lot of hurt in my twenty-five years here on this earth. If you ever get a chance to hear me speak in person or spend one-on-one time with me, maybe then you'll hear my personal testimony. Trust me when I say I got stories for days!

My brother and I have received more than enough negative criticism from people who felt that we shouldn't have written this type of book at such a young age, but I have found that the longer you hold on to things from past relationships, the more likely you are to damage present and future ones. There are people who look up to me and my ability to be as real—and oftentimes as blunt—as possible. As Christians, many people want to know that we are tangible. They want to know that we go through hardships just like everyone else, and just because we may strive to be perfect, does not mean we are. Some days I may feel like I haven't made any progress at all! I can be real because I know God has forgiven me and that I am not exempt from pain. He called me because I'm not ashamed, nor can anyone make me feel guilty for what I have done or been through.

In this book, I uncover yet another layer of myself. I know that not only am I healing, but I am hopefully helping someone else to heal. The previous book was a compilation of poetry as well, the majority of it written when my brother and I were in high school. Since then, my brother has decided to take a break from the publishing circuit in order to focus on his education and career endeavors.

I may never get to tell a lot of people that I'm sorry for what I have said or done in the past or get them to see me for all that I am today, but this is a step toward releasing years of pain that I have stored inside of me. No poem is written specifically for any one person; rather it's a mixture of emotions that I refuse to let hang over my shoulder and take with me to my grave. Jesus already did that. He died and rose for every pain and every issue. Even as I write this, I believe I am still healing.

I know without a shadow of a doubt that *My Soul on Paper II: Even Deeper* is going to bless you because it was so much of a struggle for me to reveal my innermost feelings. The closer the poems got to my heart, the more I wanted to forget this whole project! Nevertheless, I could almost see exactly what I wanted to say, as if I were reading from a scroll. The more I tried to walk away from the computer, the more drawn I felt to it. I can't tell you how many times I turned it off, only to turn it right back on again! I now know God is all over and all in this book. He gave me just the right words and scriptures in order to help free the both of us. Now, are you ready? Take my hand; let's wade even deeper.

PART I

Deeper…

Touch Me

My mind is a place you're free to caress,
A place you're more than welcome to undress
Penetrate my body and you can be replaced,
But if you penetrate my mind, thoughts of you will never
    be erased
Touch me in my most intimate spot
Stimulate my mind to the last drop
Having conversations from dusk till dawn,
I need someone in my life that is all night long

Kissing and touching can be done any day,
But I want a totally different, although much needed foreplay
You want to know what makes me happy or even cry?
Well, touching my mind gives me a different kind of high
I can guarantee that I'm nothing like anyone you'll ever come
    to know
Touch my mind and I'll never let you go

I want to know your deepest thoughts,
Share all your hopes and fears
But what happens when you come over
And I tell you that you can't stay here?
Communication is my strongest asset
And I'm as bad as I wanna be
But if I forbid the physical act of pleasure,
Can you still touch me?

I'm not easily moved by words
Because game recognizes game
However, if I can't fulfill your needs sexually right now,
Can you still say my name?

I never underestimate the power of touch
You say you can fulfill my needs, but just how much?
Enough to forego physical intimacy until our wedding day?
If I need you to touch my mind, what will you say?

But I buffet my body and subdue it, for fear that after proclaiming to others the Gospel and things pertaining to it, I myself should become unfit.—1st Corinthians 9:27 AMP

The poem you just read is one of my favorites because for the majority of my life, I've been known and most remembered for my physical attributes. Needless to say, I developed at a young age. But in defense of some of the people who have loosely described me, I put up so many walls and never gave most of them the chance to get to know the real me. All they had to go on was my physical appearance. I spent so many years making sure I kept people from invading my personal space. As a result, I attracted a lot of attention from people who wondered whether or not everything was "real."

For some reason, it seemed as if the moment I professed salvation, guys literally came out of the bushes! Maybe it had something to do with my new outlook on life or the fact that I didn't look as mean as I previously did. Beside that, I didn't know if being a church girl was the new "in" thing, but I did know that we usually got bad reputations. I had heard things like, "Church girls are the biggest freaks," and other various clichés. Nevertheless, after all of the hypocritical games I saw growing up in the church, I promised myself that I would not succumb to the desires of my flesh. And as long as God continues to encourage and support me, I will not fornicate or commit adultery. (Y'all praying for me, right?)

In a society where you are definitely in the minority if you're *not* having sex, this is much easier said than done. Sometimes I have to hug my pillow extra tight, or even throw a tantrum, but the one thing that I absolutely hate doing is wasting time. If I 'slip up' and participate in premarital sex of ANY kind (and I mean that literally), then I am prolonging my journey to my destiny. I must stay focused on the assignment that God has trusted me to fulfill. I can't afford to stare at this fork in the road and choose the wrong path.

Being focused doesn't constitute naiveté. For instance, it's not that I don't see what's going on around me; I just refuse to get distracted. Being single, saved, and possessing a passion for the ministry can often lead to an abundance of intermingled emotions. Any time you are a threat to the devil's kingdom, he makes it his business to send people to hinder you from doing what God has called you to do. He knows what you like. In my case, at different times in my life, the enemy has strategically placed men in my path that were all nearly exactly the type I asked God for. As a result, I was left with a very major decision: Either I could settle for "Mr. Right Now" or wait on God for the one He created especially for me. It hasn't always been easy, but I've been determined to be the exception.

Furthermore, I don't let my body make decisions for my spirit. With that said, I do not come across many guys who can hold a conversation that interests me. I have found that my bluntness and gift of discernment leaves most men fumbling for just the right words to say. You may be thinking that I'm saying this with a touch of arrogance, and you're absolutely right if you are! I feel that men have it too easy with a lot of women, but I'm not so desperate to be in a relationship that I'll believe or sacrifice everything for the sake of companionship.

There are so many people who pretend to be looking solely for sexual gratification in a relationship. They try to give off the *illusion* that they are happy with that type of arrangement when they find it, when in fact they aren't. I don't know why some men—and even some women—depreciate their significance down to their bodily organs. They speak highly of their expertise in pleasing members of the opposite sex, as if that is the primary reason for their existence. To say that my patience has thinned with such absurd boasting would be an understatement!

I believe that how a man approaches me is very important. If his idea of enticement is to assume that I will be in awe of his "skills" illustrated in explicit detail, then that man will be sadly mistaken. I would like to believe that by now I have heard it all, and I must say I am not impressed!

There is so much more to me than what men perceive my skill level to be in the bedroom. Like most women, I like to talk about everything and nothing at all. But what I absolutely love to do is hold stimulating, thought-provoking, soul-searching conversations. I can't speak for all women, but I am not infatuated with the illusion of happiness and prosperity. I don't want to fake being happy; I actually want to *be* happy. Due to the fact that God has allowed me to see so much with my own eyes, I have decided not to go along with the crowd. The old church mothers said it like this: "Either you're gonna come all the way in or you may as well stay all the way out, because it's either holiness or hell!"

I have heard just about every message you can think of about being single, yet sometimes I just want to be ignorant of my teachings. I don't care how saved you are or how long you've been walking with the Lord, there are going to be some times when you'd much rather do the exact opposite of what He told you to do. It is during these times that I'm faced with the one thing I cannot escape—my reflection, whether it is in my own eyes or the eyes of someone else. I'm here to tell you that the spirit of conviction ain't nothing to play with. You can try to run from it, but there will always be a small voice in your head, attempting to steer you in the right direction, whether you choose to listen to it or not. God always has a way for your escape. The scripture says, *"No temptation has overtaken you but such as is common to man; and God is faithful, who will not allow you to be tempted beyond what you are able, but with the temptation will provide the way of escape also, so that you will be able to endure it."~1st Corinthians 10:13*. Whether you actually listen to that small voice telling you to flee temptation is entirely up to you.

If you're anything like me, you spend more time at your place of employment than you do anywhere else. And you are a willing participant in all the fakeness that goes on; you wouldn't care if one of those people at work fell off the face of the earth tomorrow (ok, that's a bit extreme, but you know what I mean!). Seldom do you find people who have the same wonderful personality and optimistic attitude at home, work, school, and church. I have a low tolerance for smoke, so after the cameras stop rolling, this is who I am.

"Blessed is the man that endures temptation; for when he is tried, he shall receive the crown of life."—James 1:12

My Greatest Enemy

My greatest enemy isn't the white man,
Church folk or the people at work
It isn't my neighbors, teachers, friends or foes,
But it lies within my hurt

My greatest enemy isn't my family,
Exes or the people in my class
It is the one thing I cannot escape
My reflection in the glass

I can wear designer clothes,
From the hat on my head to the shoes on my feet
Cover my face with makeup, keep my hair and nails done
But it can only mask me

I've tried to be the life of the party,
But I cannot escape the glass
And no matter who people think I am,
I will never forget my past

I've even tried to separate myself,
Keep everyone at a distance
But no matter how many times I've prayed,
This pain is insistent

I've tried to leave my scars at the altar,
But my greatest enemy is in my house
It's in the windows, bathrooms and bedrooms,
Forcing *me* to sleep on the couch

Every time I think I'm healed,
I end up in the valley again
Taking one step forward, two steps back
Beseeching God to forgive me of my sins

As I slowly walk to the mirror,
In an attempt to see what God sees
Of all the people He could have chosen,
I can't imagine why He would set His eyes on me

I'm so ashamed of all that I have done today,
Let alone my past
God please help me to deal with me
As I turn to face the glass

I believe the most significant part of the healing process is asking God to show us who we really are. Our true identity lies underneath the designer clothes, fancy hairstyles and the Oscar-deserving performance we partake in on a day-to day basis. In other words, realizing where our pain or problems stem from is extremely crucial, after admitting, of course, that we *are* in pain or have a problem. I think I heard or read somewhere that the first step in almost any rehab program is actually *admitting* you have an addiction or problem.

Once I began to ask God to show me exactly what I was doing wrong and the underlying reason why even though I intended "to do good, but evil was always present," I must say I got scared. I began to look over my life and come to terms with why I had so many peculiar—ok, mean— ways. The reflection was enough to knock me off any high horse I may have thought I had been riding! I stopped being so judgmental when it came to people because I now realized that I wasn't automatically heaven bound. Anytime you feel the need to constantly compare yourself to other people, with you almost always having the upper hand, then there's something about you that is lacking in security, confidence and a host of other things!

Nevertheless, I think women in general need constant reassurance. Reassurance that we're pretty, loved, good mothers or cooks, and can handle our business. Some of us—myself included—lack confidence in some of those areas and seem to need someone (namely of the opposite sex) to attest to our greatness.

This next poem really digs into who I am and explains why I sometimes do the things I do. It unveils so much about me that I almost didn't publish it! I had to denounce every shred of pride to write and submit it because it's so close to my heart. The trials I went through were intricately designed to hinder me, if not stop me altogether, from attaining a reasonable level of comfort in regards to people, especially men. I didn't want people to know how vulnerable my inner being was, yet I was determined to be as transparent as possible and help somebody deal with those issues we usually won't even admit to ourselves.

No matter how much this exposition costs me in my relationships with people, I am determined to be free. I won't live my life fending skeletons. Today, I release the pain that I thought would destroy me and embrace the liberty that salvation brings.

"Now the Lord is that Spirit: and where the Spirit of the Lord is, there is liberty."—2nd Corinthians 3:17

Wanted

No masks this time around
This poem unveils my pride
No curtains, no cameras
All jokes aside

I wanted to be known for my intelligence,
But it was so much easier to be known for the curves
And even though I knew those dudes were lying,
I was a stickler for the candy-coated words

I got attention by showing off my body,
Wishing that somebody would see my heart
Wondering what I did to cause my father to run
And make me feel rejected from the start

I knew the "I love you's" were a lie;
There was no way I was the only one
So I withdrew myself emotionally
To be held and desired is what I've become

Momma's love wasn't enough
For a while I was afraid of men
Their very presence intimidated me
They couldn't even get close enough to be my friend

So I had a thing for men who were persistent,
That went above and beyond to give me some attention
Before I would look twice
His game had to be convincing

And since I'm not easily moved by gifts and trinkets,
Cars, jewelry, and oh so sweet words
The guy would literally have to go all out
To make sure my unspoken needs were heard

I wanted to be desired, pursued
After so may years of rejection and pain
Wanting men to make up for what I never had
While withholding everything but my name

Most men can tell from the way I carry myself
That I'm way beyond their reach
I'm enough trouble to catch
And even more trouble to keep

I like to think that I'm a good judge of character,
But there were times when my discernment had to be overlooked
Especially when I was being told all the right things
And I have the ability to read most people like a book

To this day I've even noticed the way I treat people,
It's an unspoken dare
Without saying what I really feel,
I'm coercing them to show me how much they care

And since I'm rarely asked my opinion,
Because everyone knows I'm real
I keep my issues buried
I want to be wanted, yet my lips are sealed

In a large crowd, you'll find me in the corner of the room
Crying on the inside, wishing I could disappear
Wanting to be happy, but being uncomfortable is what I fear

So I keep my conversation general,
Treat everyone with a long-handled spoon
Yes, it's definitely lonely,
But it's so much safer inside this cocoon

Bleeding

I feel like the world is closing in on me
I can't take this crowd
I edge my way closer to the exit,
Making excuses, saying the noise is much too loud

I absolutely HATE forced conversations
So I keep silent, taking in the view
I feel the tears getting ready to fall
As I hit the rewind to replay all of the things I have been through

I just don't know how to be happy,
So I focus on the bad
I make a beeline to my car
As people wonder how I came in smiling and left looking so sad

I can't tell them I'm bleeding,
That my bandages have come undone
Or they'll wonder what happened to me
And who's idea was it that I'd come

But I'm hurting on the inside
And the pain is taking over me
Just how many times do I have to go to the altar
In order to be free?

I rarely have advance notice
The blood just pours through my clothes,
Threatening to make me cry out
From the pain inflicted by my foes

I push away the people closest to me
By saying and assuming things I really don't feel
It would completely disrobe all that I've tried to cover
If I were to simply just keep it real

The rewind button on my past is my secret,
My excuse to spend time alone
I bring out the tissue, pen, and paper
Grab my snacks and unplug the telephone

Some people choose to shop, drink, have sex or smoke
Just to deal with the game of life
I resort to isolation
By using either fight or flight

If I don't walk away from you while you're talking to me,
Then I'll hurt you deeply with words to make you upset
Caring and asking me what's wrong
Will wind up being your only regret

I honestly don't want to care about you;
I can't afford to trust anyone else
You can't become my friend;
I have to protect myself

They say life is about taking risks with people,
But to me that's just not safe
The chance of someone hurting me
Is not a sacrifice I'm willing to make

So I'm bleeding,
Trying to keep these tears at bay
Just until I get inside my car…
Oh, why did my bandages come apart today?

My biggest problem with people
Is that I am ALWAYS misunderstood
Taking blows when I don't deserve them
Everybody thinks I'm up to something whenever I try to
   do good

So when I hit rewind
I think of all the pain I've been through
Of what it's going to cost me in the future
To accomplish the things God put me here to do

I need you to intercede for me
Even though there may have been times when I left you seething
I'm hurting behind these walls I've built with my bandages
But what can I do to stop bleeding?

Has your heart ever been broken so badly that you literally felt pains in your chest? Have you ever been hurt to the point where you couldn't even cry? My answer to both of those questions is yes. My mother always told me that whatever is in you, will come out. You can cover up behind makeup, being the center of attention, sporting the latest in designer clothes, pretending to be either aloof or passive, or you can even try your hand at being a comedian. Whatever the case may be, know that you can only play pretend for so long.

I worried about all of the pain I tried to suppress and knew that it was only a matter of time before I was bound to just go off the deep end. I didn't know whether I was going to have a nervous breakdown, become wild, or live my life on the run. I knew I needed help, and the best and only sensible thing for me to do was go back to The One who created me. That's what we all have to learn to do. For example, if you're having problems with a Lexus, then it just makes sense to go to a Lexus dealership, not just somebody that "knows about cars."

I've grown weary of the acting. All of the bitterness and anger has taken its toll on me. I'm tired of pushing people away from me. What am I going to do about it? I am going to pray, fast, forgive (you know I really need your prayers now!), and continue to study His word. I am not going to sit around and wait for happiness to fall on my lap. The world is at my fingertips. I am definitely going to live life to the fullest! I will be about my Father's business. And no, this won't make me feel free. But freedom is not a feeling; it's a state of mind.

Take inventory. Are you free or are you bleeding?

He Wins

He encouraged me not to dream, forced me to see his side
Dictated my attire, my shape I had to hide
He lied to me, hit me, and of course he cheated
It would be an understatement to say I was mistreated
Tried to convince me that no one would be as good to me as
    he was
Had me thinking what he showed me was the only true love

It hurt me, but I had to let him go
There was no need to seek revenge;
He's going to reap everything he sowed

So I had to dust myself off, let my hair down
Tear away at the wall I had built up
In order for me to let people come around

But if I seclude myself, steering away from men
Then I continue to give him power; thus, he still wins
If I develop jealous behavior based on what he's put me through,
Refusing to give myself the props that I'm due
If I allow myself to become a statistic,
Shunning the possibility of love, saying I missed it

He wins

If I continue with this pity-party, refusing to go to church
Cycles of insomnia, overeating and eventually making up
    excuses why I can't go to work
If I can just conjure up the strength to sit in the house of God,
Not simply attending for the sake of the facade
Then maybe God will hear my unspoken request
And deal with my oversized file on His desk

Maybe if I keep allowing the melody of my heart to pour into this pen
And stop deterring people from becoming my friend
Maybe, just maybe, he won't win

I *had* to succeed in college, strive to make superior grades
Become everything he said I couldn't, so that I wouldn't be sleeping in the bed he made
I wrote down my goals and fulfilled them one-by-one
And now when I look in the mirror, I see the independent woman I've become

I thought that if I engrossed myself in movies, shopping and even work,
That I could pretend I was over him, and that God had healed me of my hurt
I didn't want to admit my pain to my family and friends,
But if I don't release this baggage he left, then he still wins

Wherever he is right now,
He's reading about the real Sheree
And this poem is my first step at not letting him
Have any more power over me

"Take counsel together, and it shall come to nought; speak the word, and it shall not stand; for God is with us."— Isaiah 8:10

I'm sure you can think of a least a hundred reasons why you can't fulfill your dreams right now. It may have to do with money, lack of support from your family or friends, or your fear of failure. I don't want to live with regret, and I am determined to accomplish my dreams and not procrastinate my way through life as if I was promised forever on earth.

Try as you may, but you cannot force other people to see and respect your worth. You can tell them until you're blue in the face about how great of a person you are, but sometimes they won't acknowledge your worth until the well runs dry. I learned that the hard way.

Have you ever been associated with someone that appears to be holding one of your skeletons? It seems as if they're living life with *their* hand on *your* doorknob! Well, I have decided not to let what people think of me, stop me from doing and fulfilling my wildest dreams. I'm sure that nearly everyone who knows me or has heard my name has a "Laquania story." But God has forgiven me for what I did or said in the past and He's healing me in preparation for my future.

Hurt people know how to hurt other people. I've done and said some things that stemmed from my own insecurities, pain, and overall mean-spiritedness. I have been lied on and talked about for more years than I can count. And I have also watched and listened as my family's name was torn apart by my extended family. I didn't understand why we (my immediate family) drew so much attention. My guess is that it was because we chose to live a different lifestyle, and people generally don't like it when others set themselves apart from the crowd. It gives them reason to ridicule, and they become jealous of all the attention bestowed upon someone else and not them.

As I grew older and the disappointments and pain continued to come, the more caution tape I pulled out and the more I hated coming in contact with new people. New people meant I had to develop a new trust and comfort level. I had yet to trust and feel at ease around the people I was already associated with through blood or friendship because I figured it was only a matter of time before they would hurt me. Hence, any potential closeness increased my fear of cultivating new relationships.

To live in that fear, especially at my young age, is a terrible thing. You can't enjoy life that way. When you live your life wrapped up like a mummy, you are letting the naysayer win. How so? Well, when it comes to my place of employment, church or other venues, people have misunderstood and bad-mouthed me in the worst way. If I shut down and live my life based on fear that I will experience even more pain, then all of those negative words may as well be true. I will not do that. Instead I am going to prove them wrong by doing what they least expected me to do—dust off and move on.

"He Wins" was written from a perspective describing a relationship between a man and a woman, but let's take it even further. How many critics are 'winning' in your life? How are their doubts or insecurities affecting your decisions? Maybe you want to choose a career path that is not the norm in your family, or maybe you are interested in someone of a different nationality. Break the mold, step out of the box and do whatever it is that God wants you to do. It doesn't take a brainstorming session to come up with excuses for why we *can't* do something, but think of some reasons why you *should* start that business or go back to school, and then take the necessary steps to make it happen.

"Though thy beginning was small, yet thy latter end should greatly increase."—Job 8:7

PART II

Tea Time

In January 2007, I decided to step out of my comfort zone and become more social. Let me tell you that this was MAJOR for me because I tend to circumvent new relationships as much as I can. However, I knew that I could no longer be satisfied by waiting for someone else to implement and develop ideas to "save the world." Something was tugging at me to utilize my God-given gifts and influence to reach those wayward teens and preteens across the globe. As I sat back praying that God would use someone else, I was wasting time and my generation was taking a downward spiral.

One of the ways I chose to get involved was by joining several professional organizations. While I began the process of consulting with a few selected groups about what their organizations stood for and contributed to society, there was this one predominantly African-American association in particular that piqued my interest. However, when I inquired about their community involvement, the association had offered little to the members of the community. I was astounded that they had been around for so many years, yet had not left a significant footprint in the sand.

One of the leaders of the organization suggested that I initiate my ideas to help them give back to the community. I thought it was a good idea, but I wondered why no one else had thought about it. There we were sipping tea and eating finger sandwiches, while over half of all incarcerated individuals are minorities, many who are still anticipating the substantial dwindling—if not total elimination—of racism and discrimination. I feel that if a person is in the position to make substantial changes for the betterment of our people, then that person or group of persons should do so. For example, let's say my name could draw a large crowd or gather the support of thousands (and hopefully someday it will), then I need to use that to my advantage and do whatever is in my power to shift the world from its complacency.

Needless to say, with so much ambition inside of me, I was more than a little discouraged from joining the seemingly stagnant organization. In the meantime, I've been working on getting my issues together so I can be more comfortable speaking to and in front of people. I'm sure you've figured out by now that networking is definitely not one of my strong points . . . yet.

This section of *My Soul on Paper II: Even Deeper* invites you to join me for 'tea,' as I probe into much deeper issues instead of who was wearing what on the latest awards show, who's sleeping with whom in Hollywood and who's currently married to whose ex-husband in the church. I'm all for entertainment, but I don't have time to sit in front of the TV getting caught up on soap operas, music videos and the like. There are people hungry for the word of God, needing someone to tell them how to reach the one God who really loves them unconditionally.

I was once appalled that the aforementioned organization even asked me to have tea, but I've grown to love that soothing taste as it trickles and calms my heart, mind, soul and body. And I realize how relaxed I become as a result of drinking it. Now . . . you relax . . . and get comfortable, because we're about to really, really talk.

My Tribute

Black

The dictionary defines you in such a negative connotation
Angry, depressing, evil, just to name a few
But if they allowed me to write one page,
I would tell the world how much I love you

My eternal gratitude to you, my ancestors
Who endured the "voyage" when you weren't given a choice
To those who were tossed overboard as cargo
Those who protested our right to vote so that I could have
   a voice

Thank you for not being ashamed of your history
For persevering when they told you it'd be much safer if you quit
For instilling in me that no one could ride my back
Unless I was willing to bend it

To those of you who sacrificed your life,
Who trudged through swamps, stricken with sickness and
   disease
To those who suffered through poverty and discrimination
To those who knew freedom wasn't really free

To those of you who grabbed the hand of my generation
In order to help pull us along
Those who paved the way for us
Bestowing pearls of wisdom, encouraging us to be strong

My utmost gratitude to those of you who united with the brotherhood,
Who reached back to keep at least one boy out of the grave
To my sisters who kept their families together,
Thank you for all the sacrifices you made

I appreciate you for mentoring our young women
And teaching them to keep their legs closed
Instructing them not to fight amongst each other
And telling how much they can accomplish
When they join together as friends and not foes

Would you believe we're still making history across the globe?

I appreciate you for making sure our young men
Kept their pants from hanging down
For instilling the importance of upward mobility
Even when their fathers were nowhere to be found

To all my sisters and brothers, who braced their shoulders
Dried their tears to do whatever they had to do
Your sacrifice has not gone unnoticed
For this is my tribute to you

∽ I wrote this poem to show that you don't have to belittle another culture to magnify your own. You can magnify who you are without minimizing someone else.

Skin Deep

Long talks until the wee hours
Trinkets, cards and bouquets of flowers

You changed how I viewed Caucasian people
I realized how hypocritical my cry was that I be treated as equal
When there I was thinking that they were all the same
Stereotyping me, never bothering to get to know my name

You forced me from the depths of tunnel vision
Gave me the chance to see people for what they brought to fruition
Allowed me to see the good in people outside my race
Encouraging me to search deeper than the skin on someone's face

We studied our history
You worked to gain my trust
I minimized our relationship
Thinking there could never be an "us"

I felt I was obligated to my people
Not to stray or jump the rope
I was thinking that my soul mate was indeed a brother
And now wasn't the time to lose hope

When I focused on oppression, the inevitable glass ceiling in my world
You countered with the tales of the good Caucasian people had done, no matter what I hurled!

And though I could go on and on with reasons why I have every
    right to be angry,
You keep reminding me to go back to the fact that I asked Jesus
    to save me
In order to be forgiven, I have to forgive
So I can't continue to make you pay for what your ancestors did

Nevertheless, I'm not sure if I can handle the looks, murmurings
    and feelings of betrayal
When it comes to uplifting my race, feeling somehow I've failed

I care deeply for you,
So I must look past your skin
I'm praying that I can accept your invitation
To be more than just friends

~

Whew! Interracial dating and marriage is a very touchy subject. I almost dared myself to go there! For some reason, I attract people from other ethnicities—not just in terms of dating, but in my friendships with women as well. In these types of situations, you have to erase any of your preconceived notions about that particular culture and allow them to show and educate you about who they are as an individual. As much as we like to classify people into certain groups, there is always someone who does not go along with what we consider the norm. For example, when you buy a bag of oranges they are not all the same size. Some may be a tad bit smaller than the others. You pick the one you like best, but you know and are able to accept the fact that there are different sizes in that bag.

In a potato sack, there are also variations in size. Just because they don't all look exactly the same, you don't throw the whole bag away! If one potato ends up looking strange, you continue to peruse through the others, to make sure they all aren't rotten or spoiled. If we can be patient with fruit and potatoes, how much more should we be patient with people? I bought some grapes once that wound up not tasting so good. Know something? I didn't stop buying grapes!

There's some good in everybody. That's why it's so hard to believe those news-breaking stories of the seemingly loving wife who ended up smothering her children to death, or the father-figure coach who's been secretly molesting children. I'm sure you can think of at least one person in your past or present that you thought you knew who ended up blowing your mind!

We have to stop focusing on the bad in people and then casting judgment upon the entire race they belong to. We cannot lump people into clusters and write them off as being a certain way. Yes, I have been a victim of discrimination, but I won't let that stop me. After all of the brilliant accomplishments African-

Americans have made over the years, I can still give you scenario after scenario of the racial slurs that have been hurled at me this year alone! My stories are nowhere like the ones my forefathers could tell. Nevertheless, they are painful. Sometimes I feel as if I have every right to be angry or return the harsh treatment I have received, but I can't let those feelings overtake me. I could possibly miss out on a beautiful friendship by not embracing a person who may not share my same ancestry.

No matter how many times a person may tell you that they have no reservations about people of a particular ethnic group, I have found that a few drinks, a heated argument or a tragic event will reveal their true colors. I have dated outside my race and if it came down to it, I would do it again. I am learning that life is too short for all of the inhibitions we develop over time. Love is what love does. John 3:16 says, *"For God so loved the world that He gave His only begotten Son . . ."* When you love someone, you are acting unselfishly. It is both an action and a sacrifice. The Creator knows what I like. Therefore, I trust Him completely to choose the right man for me, no matter how dark or how light he turns out to be.

Men are beautiful, and I appreciate the creativity and artistic flair God used to create them in all shapes and colors. He is the greatest composer and I honor Him. Of all the wonderful things God created with just a spoken word, He broke the mold when He created Man—in all shades.

Then Peter began to speak: "I now realize how true it is that God does not show favoritism but accepts men from every nation who fear him and do what is right."—Acts 10:34-35 NIV

Off By a Shade

She said she liked my clothes
But pitied me because of my skin
Said that if "circumstances" were different
Then she could really see us being friends

He told me Black women were queens
As long they didn't surpass "paper bag brown"
He let me know he'd never marry me
But we could sleep around

An insider told me that if I was just a shade lighter,
I may have gotten what I thought was the ideal job
But this company was founded and operated by African-Americans
This made the news appear to be all the more odd

Come on my sisters and brothers
Don't accept that slave-like mentality
Black *is* beautiful in all its variations
And that's reality

You're not better because "you're in the house" or "in the field"
All your significant documents tell the world you're Black
And in our race for equality
It would be so much easier if we fought on the same side of the tracks

You act like you've suffered,
Singing praises about your race
But you think my skin makes me dirty
And I'm too dark to embrace

I love you my sister, my brother
Our ancestors and blood lines have already interwoven us together
Our focus should be upward empowerment and mobility,
Not which shade is better

I absolutely love Black people, and it infuriates me to no end when I hear someone making negative comments about my race, especially when that person is of the same ethnicity as I am. There are imperfections in every culture, but we have to escape tunnel vision and look at the bigger picture. I dare not resurrect the ideas and sentiments of plantation owners, slave traders and the like, in order to get you to see the damage that has plagued and continues to infest our race.

We have to redirect our focus from division to addition, adding or bringing individuals into the knowledge of the beauty of our people. I don't know what it is about our society that people always want to make themselves appear to be more superior to others. The constant need to feel superior—at the expense of someone else—is a sure sign of low self-esteem.

I'm comfortable in my skin, but I'll admit I didn't always feel that way. Somewhere between the age of ten and thirteen, I developed the concept that maybe if I was of a lighter complexion, then people would like me more. I didn't want to play outside because I didn't want to get a tan. I don't recall whether I ever voiced my concern to anyone or if anyone around me echoed my beliefs, but I took a field trip with an urban program where we followed the trail of the Underground Railroad. It was then that I began to appreciate Black people, the opposition we faced and the greater necessity to succeed. I am immensely grateful for having been given the opportunity to see my culture in a different light. The more I studied and researched my heritage, the more I loved and appreciated what my ancestors suffered to get me where I am today.

Another valuable turning point in my life came by way of one of my godmothers. She was a darker complected woman who made sun tanning her skin a recreation. Yes, she sat outside in her yard, used tanning lotion, and had no reservations about getting darker. As an adolescent of about twelve or thirteen, this shocked me. I didn't know *we* did stuff like that! However, she loved her skin tone and didn't mind taking it to the next level.

Looking back, I can't believe that there was a period in my life when I actually wanted to bleach my skin. I look at myself now and shake my head because I actually love what some people call my "walnut-complexion." I have traveled both in and out of the country, and I never regretted any of the tans I received. I love me and all that entails!

~

PART III

A Rose Among Thorns

As you may have already concluded, or will after reading further, I have had a lot of frustrations in my life when it comes to dealing with people, as I tried to make them understand who I am and why I tend to do or say things slightly different from others. As much as I have tried to conform or become the ideal Christian woman, I had to realize that I am who I am and God knew exactly what He was doing when He extended the invitation of discipleship to me. With that said, I am learning not to beat myself up, at least not as bad as I used to.

I accepted the call to the forefront on August 13, 2001, not knowing I would have to endure so much heartache and forgive people who never asked me to forgive them. The scripture says, *"Before I formed you in the womb I knew and approved of you, and before you were born I separated and set you apart, consecrating you..."—Jeremiah 1:5*. So in essence, God knew about all the issues and scars that came with my healing process. When living a Christian life, you can't expect to go from A to Z in a few months. I have gotten frustrated and upset wondering why I'm not perfect in Him, when all He wanted me to do was trust that He knows exactly what He's doing.

Oftentimes we really get messed up when we try to tell God what to do. But it's impractical for the clay to instruct the Potter. The Potter shapes the clay (I feel a preach coming on!). The scripture says, *"...Behold as the clay is in the potter's hand, so are ye in mine hand."—Jeremiah 18:6*. The clay cannot shape itself. We have to learn to "Trust God even when we can't trace God," as I once heard someone say. Your healing process is not an overnight experience. Need I remind you that you are delving into the debris we try so hard to cover up inside of us? Again, He knows what He's doing; *you* just need to get out of the way!

I am now faced with a different obstacle. A barrier created to keep me, as well as people like me, from attending and participating in church.

I have been propositioned by men in leadership positions—from pastors to deacons—ever since I was fifteen years old. And I'm talking about some anointed, talented and prophetic speakers! Oh, they could make you want to dance and speak a word so great that you knew surely no one but the Almighty had revealed it to them!

As a young woman, it was very discouraging to have to come face-to-face with church members who operated with a gift without repentance. What this means is that a person can hear from God and be godly to a certain extent, but not profess salvation and/or not be repentant or cognizant of the power and vitality of their ministry. Oftentimes, they take their gifts for granted and downplay their wrongdoings by justifying their actions.

In any case, it's a very disheartening thing to come across men in the church who use their relationship with God as a door to the bedroom. When Jesus died on the cross, the veil was torn so that I could have just as much access to His ears as the next person. I don't have to depend on someone that I feel needs to contact God for me. He didn't set aside a different telephone extension for you or me. There are no busy signals or voicemail messages necessary. I have read the Bible and I'm getting to know Him for myself.

With that said, no man can convince or manipulate me into thinking that the only way I can reach God is through him or that I need to do x to him in order for me to receive y. It is WRONG. And God will hold these men accountable for the things they have done to lead many women not to trust the men of the clergy and other lay members. In fact, the book of Ezekiel, specifically the entire thirty-fourth chapter, gives specific detail as to how God will deal with these pastors and shepherds who are responsible for His people. It is one of the most encouraging scriptures because it lets me know that He will repay those who have taken advantage of their leadership positions and caused many people to wash their hands of the whole church experience.

To those of you who have been scarred by sexual scandal and those advances that had the potential to be destructive, ask God to heal your mind. I believe the most significant gift, other than the Holy Ghost, that you can ever receive is the gift of discernment. That irreplaceable gift has steered me from a lot of useless relationships. So if I choose to ignore what God has revealed to me about certain people, then I can't blame anybody but myself.

You will encounter all kinds of people in the church, so please don't be surprised if you come across some members who encourage you not to "rock the boat" or expose the devil for who he really is. We, especially singles, are under constant attack because the enemy wants to trick us into believing that we are not complete or whole, simply due to the fact that we are not blessed with physical companionship with a member of the opposite sex. Get over it! Just because you are married doesn't mean you won't be lonely or miserable at some point. Lord knows, I know some people that . . .

Anyway, before you take that step down the aisle, you better learn how to sleep with God and be content! After all, two broken people do not equal a whole person. You see, math is a little different outside the classroom. For instance, some women give birth to children and assume that the man will marry or love them more. Having kids by someone does not equal love and marriage, especially in this day and age.

I frequent the house of God on a regular basis, and people seem to be amazed that I haven't "found" a man at church. Deacons, men in the pulpit or who play instruments don't impress me any more than the average guy on the street. I look at a person's heart and intentions toward me. I told you before: if you're patient, people will show their true colors.

They claim to know God, but by their actions they deny him. They are detestable, disobedient and unfit for doing anything good.
—*Titus 1:16 NIV*

Pray for the Prey

A mentor, confidante, spiritual guide
A hustler and a man with too many secrets to hide
He preyed upon my vulnerability, called me his friend
Now I'm left hoping that I never see him again
He preyed upon the fact that my life was a harbor of pain
And since I walked in that church three years ago, my life will never be the same

He encouraged me to share my dreams with him,
All the while planning the method for attack
I'm hurt and confused,
Wondering where was God at

I've sat at dinner with him and his wife
You couldn't have convinced me that I'd eventually have to fight
Fight to keep his hands off me, ultimately moving across town
All because of a man who preyed upon the fact that my daddy wasn't around

Who is he? The Pastor. I asked him to pray *for* me; instead he saw the prey *in* me

Grandma raised me, until I was assaulted by a neighbor
I was looking for rest for my soul in the arms of a Savior
So I set out to join this church,
Thinking that I'd escape from my hurt
I came in broken, begging the congregation to just let me sleep on the floor
I would've been better off in the streets than having the Pastor creeping to my door

He listened to me, waited until I was of age
Then tried to convince me to sleep in the bed he made

I was willing to do whatever he said to see God in peace,
All the while he was destroying my credibility

Told the church I was a thief, just because I said no
God, is there a place where broken people go?

I'm hurting all over again,
Wondering how I'm going to get through the day
I'm asking for your prayers,
Not for prosperity, but pray for the prey

—Beware of false prophets, which come to you in sheep's clothing, but inwardly they are ravening wolves.—Matthew 7:15

The Cost of the Anointing

For I reckon that the sufferings of this present time are not worthy to be compared with the glory which shall be revealed in us.
—Romans 8:18

It makes you pace the floor,
When you really wish you could sleep
Turn down your plate and fast,
When you'd much rather eat

I wish I could say every day is sunshine,
But some days you may have to crawl through the storm
You may feel like you've made the right decision,
Only to find out you were wrong

I didn't automatically know my purpose
Some days I wanted to jump ship
Throw in the towel, give up
But He told me not to quit
Oftentimes I feel blind, yet compelled to lead
To let people know that He saves and forgives
Wanting them to understand that there is a healing for their soul
Which should give them all the more reason to live

I wish I could tell them
How easy salvation is
About the love and support from church members
And that everyone will encourage you now that you are His

But people will judge, lie, and talk about you
Right in the church
Some days you won't feel like turning the other cheek
And loving the very person who caused you to hurt

Some members will be intimidated by your gifts
They'll constantly look for flaws
There'll be times when you feel like you don't measure up
Even when you know that you've given your all

You may have to sit or work
With the very person who brought you pain
Forced to forget the tears you've cried
And what they've done to destroy your good name

But all of the misunderstandings, the trials you face
The suffering you have to go through in order to win this race
The temptations, oh temptations,
That make you want to forget the promise you made to God
The desire to stay in your comfort zone and hide behind the
    façade

All of this is making you,
And trust me when I say it'll all be worth it
To hear the Lord say,
"Well done, thou good and faithful servant."

Living saved is H-A-R-D! In all my years in and out of the church, I have never heard anybody admit that. Getting saved was the easy part. But life thereafter . . . whew! However, there's an old adage that says something to the effect that anything worth having is worth fighting for. My purpose in saying this is not to challenge or dispute your religious beliefs because His word is not debatable. Herbert Prochnow said, "Some people want a religion that will make them feel respectable but not require them to be." Think on that.

If you're going to live this life the way He intended, you have to brace yourself for opposition, which can come from all directions. What makes salvation so hard is that sometimes—if not most times—you're going to want to reach back to handle things the way you used to. This may include fighting, cursing people out, and seeking revenge. The things you used to do for money, you can't do anymore. All of the lies you told, the schemes, the predilections you may have had for the opposite sex, etc., are not supposed to be a part of your renewed mind.

I don't know why people in church sit up and act like being a sinner was so bad and they were so miserable. I heard a preacher say that if it was that horrible, then why do people keep going back to it? Why is it so hard to get people to convert? For me, living in sin wasn't that bad, but I had too many self-destructive behaviors. The way I was going, it was only a matter of time before I was either dead or in jail. I was unhappy and I lacked motivation to do more than just get through the day. Nevertheless, now that I've given my life over to the Lord, my greatest struggle is letting go of the old me.

What keeps me going is the fact that my heart wants to be saved. Once you get touched by God, you can never truly be the same. He keeps me saved, encourages me just when I think I can't make it another day and is patient with me when I don't get it quite right. My mom always told me, "He'll keep you, if you want to be kept." At first I didn't know what she meant by that, but now I do. If you really want to be saved, hold on; He will help you even when you can't help yourself. Every tear I shed, every cheek I had to turn and everything I had to give up was worth the peace and love I have right now. I have been in situations where a part of me wanted to give up on being a Christian, but deep inside, my heart was pleading with God not to let me go. Know something? He hasn't.

"When I said, My Foot slippeth; thy mercy, O Lord, held me up."
—*Psalms 94:18*

The Kingdom Has Need of You

I know you think you're worthless
Someone else can easily take your place
You've sinned time and time again
In church, you're too ashamed to show your face

You think that God couldn't possibly want you
There's so many people that haven't committed half the sins
    you've done
Yet the kingdom still has need of you
Look at all of the obstacles you've managed to overcome!

You've taken blow after blow
Of life's ups and downs
You've withstood the criticism
Even held on when there wasn't a friend to be found

I know that there were times when you had to cry yourself
    to sleep
When worry and pain would not allow you to keep your seat

You've said some things you wished you could take back
Done some things you hoped the world will never know
And the people you thought would be your friends
Turned out to be your foes

In the Bible:

Paul was a murderer
Solomon had hundreds of concubines and wives
Rahab obtained favor, even though she was a harlot
David slayed so many lives

God used and forgave them

There's no way you can undo the things you've said or done
Yet, God is calling you to redeem the time
He forgives even when people refuse to forget
For your sin is no greater than mine

Someone needs to hear your story
There are so many souls you can win
People are unknowingly waiting on you
You've *got* to let them know that Jesus forgives all sins!

You can't expect to get by on "God knows my heart"
Today can be a new start!

What if you don't make it another day?
What will you do?
Don't you know the kingdom has need of you?

"And after you have suffered a little while, the God of all grace, who has called you to His eternal glory in Christ Jesus, will Himself complete and make you what you ought to be, establish and ground you securely, and strengthen, and settle you."
—*I Peter 5:10*

The pity-party, God won't forgive me, I don't deserve anything good to happen to me, and I'll take what I can get are the most common tricks the devil likes to play. I was a victim of that same manipulation at least a hundred times. Even as I write this, I am struggling with the immense calling God has placed on my life. Sometimes I feel inadequate, as if I am not able to live up to the standard He desires in each of us. I feel I've done so much that couldn't have possibly been pleasing in His sight.

I think the most powerful button on a stereo system is the rewind button or, more recently, the arrow that allows you to go back to a certain part in a particular song. But the second most powerful button is "play." Play on a tape player (shame on you if you still have one!) allows you to begin from your current place. Today, I encourage you to pick up where you left off. I urge you to *"...forget those things which are behind, and reach forward unto those things which are before, I press toward the mark for the prize of the high calling of God in Christ Jesus."—Philippians 3:13-14*. It doesn't matter what song played prior to this one. You can start over. Today can be the first day of the rest of your life. I don't know if you remember the part in the poem you just read that says, *He forgives even when people refuse to forget.*

So much of our fear of the future has to do with our past. Most of us have a fear of failure. For example, there are some entrepreneurial ideas that I would love to pursue right now, but I do not want to fail. Someone asked me, "What would you do if you knew you could not fail?" That question opened up so many doors in my mind. If there was no chance I could fail at something, then I'd be sprouting up businesses across the globe! I have been putting it off for far too long. Nevertheless, slowly but surely, I am getting away from the fear that has kept me from fulfilling my wildest dreams. Now, can I ask you that question? What would *you* do if you could not fail?

There is a whole world out there that needs to hear our testimonies. One of the steps I am taking to rid myself of fear is writing this book. People have told me that poetry doesn't sell and that maybe I should try to write something else. That is not where God has led me, so I have to follow my own inner voice for the time being. Selling books is a perk, but not my sole reason for writing. I like to write in general, but poetry is my passion because it unveils much of what I try so hard to hide. People can barely handle my poems, let alone if I were to write a fictional book! It would definitely not be for the faint hearted! Nonetheless, I love to write and I'm full of surprises, so who knows what I'll think of next?

I said all that to say this: your testimony is crucial. You will not only free yourself, but you will free someone else that may be staring at the same hurdle you once thought you'd never get over. That person may feel like victory is too far away and your testimony may be just what he or she needs to make that leap. I know because I have read the e-mails and received the phone calls from people who informed me that my testimony helped them tremendously. People were inspired to know that they, too, could write a book or pursue an idea that they'd been toying with for years. These words of encouragement propelled me to write a second book. It forced me to continue the healing process, even though there were so many times when I wanted to walk away from God. But like I told you before, once you have been touched by Him, it is impossible to remain the same.

I beseech you to ask God to forgive you for what you have done. Forgive yourself for whatever God has already cast into the sea of forgetfulness. If you keep standing in the same place, life will pass you by and before you know it, you'll be in the Judgment line. One of the hardest things for me is moving on after someone has hurt me, but I don't have time to stand still. I want to be happy. I want to be free. I want to be healed. Those are the things that keep me from turning my back on God or freezing up and becoming too comfortable with wherever I may be at a particular time. It doesn't take a strong person to stay in one place, but it takes someone of extreme substance to keep marching, no matter how many storms come or how many blows they may have to take. There is a war going on, and I'm in it to win it.

"... *For he that cometh to God must believe that he is, and that he is a rewarder of them that diligently seek him.*"—Hebrews 11:6

I've experienced a whole lot of pain in my short life. In spite of it all, I still believe that God has created someone just for me. Yes, me, with all my issues; I believe that somebody out there wants a 'subscription' (heyyy!). I have enough sense to believe that no one is perfect, but no amount of pain will convince me to give up on the love God designed to exist between a husband and wife. People are always trying to convince me to settle, but I have spent most of my life settling. I settled for a *C* throughout elementary school, high school and the first half of college. I settled for the companionship of a man who refused to commit, and I even settled for minimum-paying jobs. Some time after, I accepted Christ as my Lord and Savior and decided that I deserved more. As a result, I didn't even know *how* to settle anymore.

Don't let the devil deceive you into believing that you don't deserve nice things or for good things to happen to you. God forgives, but we have to learn to forgive ourselves. Yes, it's hard because we are our greatest enemy. What makes the Bible so great is that it contains a plethora of stories of imperfect people who obtained God's favor in spite of who they were or what they'd done.

I don't know what it is about us as people that we can conjure up every reason why we feel we don't deserve this or that because of something that God has already forgiven us for. If you allow yourself to constantly hit rewind and focus on all of the 'bad' things you've done throughout the course of your life, then you'll never be happy, nor will you be able to receive the blessings God has in store for you (that word was for both you and me).

Now that I'm off the soap box, I don't know what it is about me that I always seem to attract the wrong types of guys. When I divulged to one of my cousins about being approached by married men and men who have girlfriends, he enlightened me with something that never crossed my mind. He told me, "The reason you are approached by committed men is that those men who are 'taken' have nothing to lose if you reject their advances. A single guy is easily intimidated by your accomplishments and don't-take-no-mess attitude." He finished by saying that overall I didn't give off a look of desperation." I walked away from him not feeling so bad. I became secure in knowing that I didn't have a sign above my head that read, "I WILL BE YOUR MISTRESS." I deserve more than that.

In fact, I deserve so much more that I've decided to let the world know that even at the age of twenty-five, I still believe in fairy tales. No one is perfect, but there is someone that has been intricately designed by God just for me. And God has managed to heal and conceal my scars so that it looks like I haven't experienced so much pain. I am and will continue to be a rose . . . even among thorns.

"*. . . Not one thing hath failed of all the good things which the Lord your God spake concerning you; all are come to pass unto you, and not one thing hath failed thereof."—Joshua 23:14*

I Still Believe in Fairy Tales

I still believe in fairy tales
Despite all I've been through
I believe God has set aside someone just for me
And they'll do whatever they gotta do
If that means work two jobs
To provide for us
And putting his pride aside
In order to gain my trust

I still believe in fairy tales
Someone is going to sweep me off my feet
He'll be everything that I've asked God for
And do what it takes to please me

Even though I've met so many unfaithful men,
I still believe in fairy tales
And although no relationship is perfect,
I believe true love never fails

It seems like society promotes unfaithfulness,
But I still have this twinge of hope left inside of me
That there is at least one good man left
That will not compromise his loyalty

I still believe in fairy tales
I've chosen how I want to live
To fall in love or settle?
I dare not take what these men give

I've come across so many men
Who tell me I'm the only one
Yet within a matter of weeks, if not days
The lies have already begun

A cheating man is not worth my time
I can't stand a man who won't work
An abusive, controlling, selfish man
Shouldn't bother stepping to me with his dirt

I'll wait on God to fulfill His promise
Even though it's not easy being alone
Some days are harder than others
It's an ever present struggle to not reach for the phone

But with all of the hype about down low brothers
And the ones that are lazy, ungrateful, cheating, or even in jail
I know I'm a good woman, and for some reason
I still believe in fairy tales

Expensive

I know you're used to exchanging combo meals for sex
Only stayed in relationships long enough to get your feet wet
You're used to lying and wearing women down to get your way
Showing them that in order to enjoy your company, they'll have to pay

Pay with their common sense
The little voice demanding to know what the "friendship" is really about
Never having to iron your lies, Mr. Casanova
Using your candy coated words and magic hands to make sure the jury stays out

You're used to approaching sassy women
With little or no self-esteem
Women who'll sacrifice their standards for companionship
It's to your advantage that Daddy never was on the scene

You're used to coming and going as you please
I'm here to tell you that you've finally met your match
When you decided to step to me!

You took one look at me and accepted the challenge
Said, "This'll be easy," you so quickly assumed
Knew that you'd have to pull out all the stops
To get me into your bedroom

But I saw you coming from a mile away
Finished your sentences, paid for my own check
It was getting late, so I bid farewell
After all, we had only just met

Your car, suit and passion for the ministry
Made you look good,
But your spirit didn't move me

You see, I'm expensive
To be with me is going to take time and definitely some work
I have my own money, house and car
And I'm not impressed with how many times you go to church

I can be subtle or feisty, bourgeois, but real
Soft as velvet or as cold as steel

You need to spend time with God
In order to get past these walls I've built for miles
And I'm not saying 'I do' until I'm whole
So there's no need for me to rush down the aisle

Don't just tell me; you have to show me
That you mean what you say
I know what you're used to,
But with me, there'll be a whole lot of times you won't get
   your way

Yes, I'm calling you out
Step up your game and lose some of that chauvinistic pride
Because you're not bringing anything to the table emotionally
And about the smallest things, you lie

I'm expensive, so can you put in the work?
You can flash money, but can you get past my hurt?

PART IV

He Didn't Deserve Me

Never Say Never

Roses every Friday,
Cards just because
Cologne scented letters,
Long talks about falling in love

For six months he pursued me,
Passionate, I must say
Intrigued me to pay closer attention to him
When I originally said I would never give him the time of day

He went out of his way to take me to work
Even waited while I was in class
Such a gentleman
Even respected my space when I felt we were moving too fast

We got married and I felt as if I was on a three year high
Now, what I wouldn't give for the strength to say goodbye

I always said that I would only get married once
Would never accept any form of abuse
Now I've learned never to say never,
Especially now that I've walked in several different shoes

He never strikes me when the kids are around
And now I've learned how to muffle my screams,
Not make too much of a sound
He hits me, but he's faithful
And it's not like it's every day
We're comfortable, and one day I'll leave him
Just please, not today!

I have to think about our kids
And we've built so much together
I don't want to start all over again,
Even though I know I deserve better

I wasn't raised to divorce when things get rough
We vowed until death do us part
And he hasn't broken anything
Just my spirit . . . and maybe my heart

I was raised without a father
I don't want my kids to have to experience that life
And even though we're going through a little something
    right now,
I made a commitment to be his wife

I said he would never break a bone
My face he'd surely save
But be careful to never say never,
Because now I speak from the grave

"Ye husbands, dwell with them according to knowledge, giving honor unto the wife, as unto the weaker vessel, and as being heirs together of the grace of life; that your prayers be not hindered."
— 1st Peter 3:7

Domestic violence is a recognized generational curse in my family. Although my mother didn't experience physical abuse, it still affected me. My extended family (aunts, cousins, etc.) were victims of domestic violence. I grew up resenting and feeling the utmost pity for them because they had once been my role models. These women were beautiful and full of potential, yet they chose to stay committed to men who brought them and their children so much pain.

Due to the fact that my mom ran a very strict household and did not have strange men—or any man other than an occasional visit from an uncle—around us, I never knew what a woman was supposed to be treated like by the opposite sex. People can tell you all day what you should or should not accept, but to actually go through the motions makes all the difference. Not having that opportunity, I could have carried on the generational curse and tolerated abuse from a man; however, God blessed me, and I have never personally experienced domestic violence.

Even so, with any relationship, there is bound to be some confrontation. Now that I look back, there could have been some instances where things escalated for the worse. I don't think I am above getting abused in that way, because we have all done some things and allowed some things to happen that we said we would NEVER accept. (Can the church say Amen?) At this moment, I can't imagine domestic violence ever being my testimony, but instead of saying never, I say, "God, I hope you keep me loving myself enough to not allow someone to abuse me."

I refuse to believe it's God's will for us to be treated like tissues instead of vessels. Recognize how valuable you are. You have to love yourself. When you truly love yourself, you won't allow someone to play tennis—or in some cases, dodge ball—with your heart. When I began to really look in the mirror and saw that I was indeed fearfully and wonderfully made (Psalms 139:14), not just on the outside, but on the inside as well, I stopped making excuses for not being treated the way a woman should be treated. I realized that every time a man walked out on me or didn't commit, it wasn't solely my fault. God allowed me to see that it wasn't that the man was too good for me. Some guys just couldn't handle the call that had been placed on my life, and I may not have been the best person to serve as a help mate in theirs. Whatever the case may be, God, I'm *so* glad that you rescued me!

Oftentimes when someone does not want to be with us, we automatically beat up on ourselves. Am I too fat? Am I too skinny? What I had to realize is that there are indeed some areas where I could use improvement, but once again I am fearfully and wonderfully made. I had to see myself as a beautiful queen first in my own eyes before I expected someone else to. So instead of always assuming that there was something wrong with me, I had to admit that some men can't handle women like me. I'm worth it all and ain't scared to tell you!

We get so caught up in the mundane walk of life that sometimes we want to stop the charade and have someone see who we really are behind the mask. I, for one, have some days when I just want to jump up and down and say, "Look at me! I'm here!" For instance, there was this guy I was interested in, but he didn't seem to notice me. He was droning on and on about someone else and meanwhile I was thinking, *What's wrong with me?* I didn't know him that well, but a light bulb went off in my head and I said to myself, *Am I invisible?* If he couldn't see the diamond that clearly stood before him, then I figured it was best that I let him continue his search through the bushes! Heyyy!

We shouldn't be so quick to write ourselves off like we're not good enough for someone else. God could be keeping you away from a potential heartache or a waste of time altogether. So thank Him for steering you away from certain people or for the rejection from others. You are somebody special, and after all you have gone through to get where you are today, you deserve more.

You Didn't Deserve Me

On my knees I prayed that I would heal
I pleaded with God to make you experience the pain I feel
I thought that we'd be good together
But since you've betrayed me, I know I deserve better

Usher had his turn; it's time I make my own confession
I don't regret meeting you; it was truly a worthwhile lesson

My friends weren't enough for you; you even slept with my foes
And there I was wishing that I didn't know

I kept retracing my steps, wondering where I went wrong
Was the wig too short, my real hair too long?

Was I too skinny?
My life too public?
In spite of it all, I can't say I didn't see it coming

I had all the warnings; I never missed the signs
Yet I still fell for a man that wasn't mine

I had been blaming myself, wondering why you couldn't see
    my worth
Until I began to tell God how much it hurt

He then began the process
Of restoring my joy
I never knew I had so much strength,
Until you treated my love like a toy

I stayed in the mirror,
Hoping that there'd be something about me that would catch your eye
But instead your actions made it so much easier
For me to say goodbye

You didn't deserve me

A young, educated Black woman
Classy enough for your arm
Fly, yet humble
With just enough sass not to cause too much harm

Once I stopped blaming myself
For all that you could not see,
I came to my senses and realized
YOU DIDN'T DESERVE ME

Midnight Girl

Ten o'clock phone call
By eleven he's at the door
He doesn't know it,
But I'm planning to tell him I can't do this anymore

I allow him to vent about his day,
Convincing myself to stand my ground
Repeating to myself that I need more
Than temporary this time around

He initiates contact
And I'm sure I can't win
Thought I would give him 'the speech,'
But now I'm in the sheets again

I can't sleep, so I get up,
Even though I really planned to be strong
When I look back at him,
I know that what we're doing is wrong

He doesn't want to commit
No immediate plans to take that trip down the aisle
I'm not good enough to marry,
But he wants me to have his first child?!

I can't stand to look in the mirror,
After all that I have done
I know I'm better than this,
But look at what I've become:

A Midnight Girl
I can't tell him he's hurting me,
Or he'll bring me gifts in return
I'm infatuated with him,
And I can't just let it burn

I want him to really see me,
Appreciate my worth
But I keep quiet,
Shielding the very appearance of hurt

What's a midnight girl like me to do,
When I don't feel worthy of love?
I allowed myself to be sexed,
When all I really wanted was a hug

"Stand fast therefore in the liberty wherewith Christ hath made us free, and be not entangled again with the yoke of bondage."
—*Galatians 5:1*

How many life-changing decisions were made based on a one-night stand? Have you put yourself at risk of disease by having unprotected sex? Was there a child created with someone you thought you'd never see again? I know we exist in a day and age where we live for the moment, but we—especially women—need to realize that one night can change your whole life. I deserve more than one night. In fact, I am so special that I deserve forever!

I'm not waiting for some man to leave his wife or girlfriend and make a commitment to me. It makes no sense for us to justify someone's infidelity in order to convince ourselves it will never happen to us. We've all heard the saying, "If he cheated *with* you, he'll cheat *on* you." Now that may not be true in every case, but let's just say I never knew of a relationship resulting from an affair that lasted.

As a single Christian woman, I'm supposed to wait on God to send my husband to find and pledge me as his wife, promoting celibacy all the way. Now, lean in and listen closely: It is extremely difficult to honor this promise to God (especially if you're just going to say, "God knows my heart," and sin anyway) because He created us with desires. Those desires don't just go away when you give your life to God. Cold showers, group Bible studies, jogging and shopping don't always work. Sometimes you may have to get down on your knees and pray until you can't pray anymore, cry yourself to sleep, or in some cases, simply flee the potential crime scene! One night with the wrong person can lead to days, weeks, months, or years of regret and guilt—maybe even child support!

You have to know your limitations. If you know you usually start talking crazy by nine p.m., then you need to be off the phone no later than eight-thirty. If you can't handle being on a one-on-one date because the chemistry is too strong, then you need to stay in groups and have someone hold you accountable for your whereabouts. It can be a bit irritating and infantile, but if you're going to do this thing the right way, then you gotta do what you gotta do, by any means necessary. Don't set yourself up to fall. God will make a way for your escape.

I adorn myself and my house with reminders of my endeavor to uphold a real Christian, single life. I keep a note plastered on my dresser that says, *It's not worth my anointing, not even for a few minutes.* I have anointed the walls of my house with blessed oil (oil that has been prayed over) so I have a constant reminder of the God that lives inside of me (because we're quick to tune that small voice out!), and other things that have been strategically placed around me to make me feel guilty and completely halt me from making a wrong and very costly decision.

It took me a long time to get where I am today and I am not just talking dollars and cents. I'm speaking of the Laquania Sheree who actually loves herself. I can honestly say that I love God so much that I dare not hurt Him by following my own agenda. He loved me when I couldn't bring myself to look in the mirror. I've made and broken promise after promise to Him, yet He still didn't push me aside. For that I am immensely grateful. Because I've shed my once low self-esteem and valued the unconditional love God has shown me, my tolerance for a lot of useless nonsense has reached an all time low.

If I fill my plate up with food I like, then I won't have room to add more items that I won't be able to eat. With that said, if you get your life together and continue to fill your plate with things you enjoy doing, there will be less time spent on twirling your circumstances in circles like we do our food. You will also be less susceptible to people dumping their problems on your plate. You deserve more. Now act like it!

"Blessed is the man that endures temptation: for when he is tried, he shall receive the crown of life, which the Lord hath promised to them that love him."—James 1:12

He Wants Me to Wait

He says I'm the one for him
Without a shadow of a doubt, we should be together
He says he married the wrong person
And that things will soon get better

So my guess is that I'm supposed to cross my fingers
And pray that I'll someday have my turn
And with the issue of premarital sex of any kind,
I shouldn't be so firm

He wants me to wait

He says we share a connection
And what we have doesn't happen every day
But no matter how much it hurts me,
God's will is what I pray

I don't believe He would give me
Someone that I would have to share with someone else
And if it really is true love,
Then why am I hurting
And second guessing myself?

If he cheats on her, why would he hesitate to cheat on me?
Is a question that haunts my mind
I don't have the strength or the patience
To be second to another woman one more time

He wants me to wait until things blow over
But take a good look at me
I'm too good of a woman to be in this situation
So please just let me be

My philosophy is: handle your business *before* you step to me
Because I bring a whole lot to the table
How could you possibly care for me,
And at the same time give me the 'Number 2' label?

I'm a faithful, giving, and honest person
Not to mention saved
And all these years I've waited for my husband to be,
I've felt compelled to behave

But now I've met this man
Who wants me to wait
He doesn't want me to be with anyone else
And our "once in a lifetime connection"
Has become his bait

However, you don't meet people like me every day
I have beauty that comes from the inside out
I had no idea he would treat me like this
And that goodbye would come out of my mouth

To think he wanted me to wait

Be not deceived; God is not mocked: for whatsoever a man soweth, that shall he also reap.—Galatians 6:7

I wrote the next poem because I was tired of struggling with whether to pray for a certain guy or begging God to make my enemy my footstool. Put yourself in my shoes: imagine living in an apartment building with someone you felt like you had a connection with, dealing with seeing that person nearly every day, and finding out that he is 'connecting' with everybody! It hurts to pray for someone that you feel doesn't deserve God's unmerited favor. It's funny, because if I allow myself to be honest, I don't deserve at least half of the favor God has blessed me with! I'm so glad that favor isn't fair!

Furthermore, He holds us accountable for doing what He has called us to do. Who am I to question whether or not someone *deserves* my prayers? I ought to be grateful that God hears *me* at all! I may not have done the things to the extreme that the guy I spoke of earlier with the whore-like tendencies has done, but no sin is greater than the other. I'm guilty of a whole lot of stuff. You're curious, right?

Well for starters, I can be extremely . . . uh . . . mean. Yep, shocking, I know. So, if I don't get this "love your enemies" thing together and the guy keeps fornicating, we'll both be in big trouble on Judgment Day!

I said all that to say this: the Bible says in Romans 12:21, *"Do not be overcome by evil, but overcome evil with good."* As I prayed for God to untangle me from that situation, it actually helped me to release hurt and anger. I felt better and the things my neighbor had done to me, whether they were intentional or not, no longer had the power to change my day for the worse. He didn't have that power he once had over me. As I was living my life in utter distaste for his mere existence (ok, I hated him!), I wasn't allowing God to heal me. He could still go on with his life, repent, find a wife and live happily ever after, and there I was relishing in my strong dislike for him treating me less than I felt I deserved.

Look at how much time we've wasted asking God to make people pay for the way they treated us. I told you all before: the best way to get back at somebody is to go on with your life. The earth does not stop moving because someone hurt your feelings. At the time, it may feel like the end of the world, but you can look around you and see that Paris is still Paris, the sun is still shining and you are the one that's replaying all of that pain. Your healing could take years (ask me how *I* know!), but you will heal. Some days the wound may feel fresh, as if the situation just happened a few moments ago. You'll think you've been delivered and instead, get hit with a reality check. But right this moment, I am rooting for you, cheering you on and telling you that God can do ANYTHING. You can and will get through this.

I read or heard somewhere that when you hold on to a lot of ill feelings, such as hatred and the inability to forgive, then it can make you physically ill. I believe that is true, because Lord knows I have had my share of sick days! Yes, I'm still hurting, but now I pray that the young man develops a heart, not on the yellow brick road, but on the path to righteousness. It has taken a lot out of me, but now I even pray... for his healing.

"Marriage is to be held in honor among all, and the marriage bed is to be undefiled; for fornicators and adulterers God will judge."
—Hebrews 13:4

The Tin Man

I hate him for hurting me
But when I look at him, scars are what I see
So it's a struggle, a constant tug of war
I thought he was feeling me, but he treats me like a whore
He's the tin man—cold—I know he doesn't care
I thought I could reach his soul, but his heart wasn't there

I asked God to make him suffer
Instead He tells me to pray
For him?
When you're interceding for a tin man,
What exactly are you supposed to say?

As I head toward the parking lot,
I try to conjure up a smile
And with each small step, my legs feel like lead
And the journey seems like miles

You don't know how bad it hurts
He says I'm every man's dream girl,
But failed to respect my worth

I know he's not the one
Yet, a woman fed up
Is what I've become

I'm praying for someone that doesn't care if I die
He's emotionless, withdrawn
And right to my face he lies

His actions make him the tin man,
But I can hear him crying out for help
How could I have expected him to love me
When he doesn't first love himself?

I cry because deep down
My spirit is trying to resist
I want to forget about him,
But his eyes are what I miss

So God, it doesn't matter that he's been after my sister, co-worker, and neighbor
But am I still supposed to tell him the good news about the Savior?

When I see him,
I never know how I'm going to react in advance
I really want him to suffer,
But even I need the God of a second chance

This morning at the mailbox I thought I was cool,
Until I smelled his cologne
I know he's trying to be friendly,
But I wish he'd leave me alone
I get on my knees praying
He'll reap everything he's sown

God tells me to change my prayer
But all I can think about is Tamika, Diamond, Sadie, and Kim
Yet God keeps reminding me
That this tin man belongs to Him

I'd rather curse him out,
But I know even the tin man needs a hug
And I'm left with no other choice
Than to exercise His unconditional love

I keep trying to distance myself,
But his pain keeps tugging at me
There's a war going on inside my head
I really want him to suffer,
But I know he needs to be free

He's got me second guessing myself
Maybe if I'd slept with him, he wouldn't want anybody else
Ladies, how many times have we told ourselves this lie?
He knows I can see right through him,
So he avoids my eyes

How much do I really know?
Too much, but I still can't let you go
I'd much rather see you reap or get you to make me understand
Of all the guys in this world,
Leave it to me to fall for a tin man

But still . . .

I pray for your healing and your peace of mind
I pray that you've hurt me for the last time
I pray that you'll surrender and tell God yes
I even pray that your latter days will be greater than the rest

God hears you; please just take His hand
It hurts me to say this,
But know that Jesus can do anything
He can even forgive a tin man

Love your enemies, bless them that curse you, do good to them that hate you, and pray for them which despitefully use you, and persecute you; That ye may be the children of your Father which is in heaven: for he maketh his sun to rise on the evil and on the good, and sendeth rain on the just and on the unjust. If you only love those who love you, what reward will you get?
—Matthew 5:44-45

He Cut Me Loose

There were times when I thought he was feeling me
We spent so much time making each other laugh
I thought we would be good together
And that he'd make me his better half

But God allowed me to dream about him
Yes, this wonderful man of mine
He showed me who he really was
And to stay with him would be a waste of my time

I didn't want to believe Him
After all, anyone could change
I used so many excuses and justifications
Yet things could never be the same

For God held me accountable
For the visions and the dreams
Some have already come to pass
And though it hurt to see and hear the truth
"Why me?" is what I asked

But Jesus loved me enough
To spare me the pain
Of being with someone that would eventually
Bring me to an open shame

I had to forget about our long talks
And how he made me feel
I had to listen to what God had to say
Because His warnings were real

God cut me loose
Because I didn't have the strength to walk away
So He allowed him to hurt me so badly
That there was no way I could allow him to stay

God is good. We ask for so much in our prayers that oftentimes we end up contradicting ourselves. For example, we ask God to bless us with a good man. When the man we choose (because we are too impatient to really wait on God) turns out to be not so great, we ask God to heal our hearts by making him change into our Prince Charming. This is why sometimes He has to cut us loose, because we won't get rid of the person that's ruining our happiness. So He allows the person to hurt us to the point that there is NO WAY we can allow him or her back into our lives. It's painful, but necessary.

Think of a time when you chose to stay in a situation with a person you knew was no good for you. If you're honest with yourself, you can think of at least ten signs that clearly suggested you walk—or run!—away from that situation or person, but you didn't. We plead and plead with God to make us whole and get us to the level He desires for us, but He is not going to allow us to drag that baggage through life.

Currently, when you get on an airplane, the airline only allows you to bring so much weight on the flight. If your luggage surpasses that weight, then the airline charges a fee. Life with God is the same way. You can go deeper in Him to some degree, but there is a fee if you want to hang on to the past. The fee may cost you your life, relationship or growth in God, and even your sanity. You have a choice to make. What are you going to do? Is the past worth lugging around? Bag lady or bag man, don't you miss your bus!

PART V

A Day in the Life

In My Shoes

She wants to wear my shoes,
Thinking that her life would be so much better
If she could just be Laquania for a while
And have it all together

She wonders . . .

If she could just take back her promiscuity
And have a honeymoon that's all a surprise
Work the hourglass figure
And bat these pretty, dark brown eyes
If she could just forget the weave and comb long, healthy hair
Not have to dress so provocatively
In order to get men to stare

She wonders . . .

If she could be self-confident
And lose the extra weight,
Then maybe men would want her, too
And my place she wouldn't have to try and take

What she doesn't know . . .

I fought for everything I have
I have so many internal bruises, wounds, and scars
That some days I worry myself sick
And I don't want to leave the house at all

I have to constantly weed out the men
That just want to sit up in my house and push my ride
They've never gotten to know me
Or ever really looked into my eyes

I have to be conscious of the women
The ones who love to hate
Especially the ones who don't know the blessing in giving
Instead, they're just so quick to take

Every day I wrestle with my own demons,
Struggling just to do the right thing
While wondering if I can hold on
And keep Jesus as the reason why I sing

I gotta tell myself that I'm beautiful
In spite of the wounds I see
So deeply fashioned and entwined
Into whom I've already come to be

I yearn to be trusting and social,
But I've been hurt too many times
And although she wants to wear my shoes,
She wouldn't last a day in my mind

God has given me a gift
To see what would make some people run
And though I look good on paper
A living testimony is what I've really become

So even if she wants to wear my shoes,
The grass isn't always greener on the other side
You will never be able to handle
All that comes with the scars I hide

Be careful of what you pray for

I keep coming into contact with people who, for whatever reason, seem to think I got it made. Yes, I have accomplished a great deal in less than a quarter of a century here on earth, but there is a cost to all that God has blessed me to achieve. I fought for my position. What do I mean by this? I'm glad you asked! I fought in order to:

- Not allow myself to listen to the devils' insistence that I commit suicide
- Overcome the criticisms of my family and older people that I automatically assumed would shower me with words of wisdom
- Encourage myself due to the fact that life doesn't come with a cheerleading squad
- Stay in shape
- Pursue a higher education, even when teachers tried to discourage me
- Abstain from promiscuity and other self-destructive activities, etc.

I wasn't blessed with a silver spoon in my mouth. I saved my money and relied on God for whatever luxuries I've attained. Contrary to popular belief, I don't have everything. Healing, salvation and peace is something that can't be bought online. Because of the great level of anointing on my life, I am faced with an unrelenting opposition in the church (because that's where the devil is really working these days), as well as in my day-to-day life.

I learned not to be jealous of people, especially those in Hollywood, because I don't know what it took for them to get where they are. I think Lisa Raye and Gabrielle Union are very pretty (come on, give them what's due!), but anytime you're given something—and in both of these women's cases, beauty and talent— there is a cost associated with that gift, whether it's jealousy, haters, men who expect you to sleep your way to the top, and people who treat you like you think you're too good. I can imagine that Lisa Raye and Gabrielle Union have to project their inner beauty even more as a result of their outer beauty.

With that said, you must understand that the grass isn't always greener on the other side. Sure, I would love to be married to Morris Chestnut or Christian Keyes (let's give God a moment of silence out of respect for His handiwork!), but I can't fathom what their individual personalities would be like when the cameras are off. Furthermore, when you see someone driving a nice car and portraying what you consider to be the perfect life, you don't know what it's like for that person behind closed doors.

You want to have a well-toned body? Put the donuts down! You want to drive a nice car? Improve your credit, save your money and GO GET IT! I'm not encouraging you to spend or live beyond your means, but so much of what we envy in others is attainable for us! Our Father has equipped us with everything we need. What's holding you back?

The LORD said, "If as one people speaking the same language they have begun to do this, then nothing they plan to do will be impossible for them."—Genesis 11:6 NIV

Polished

She wants to know who I am wearing skirt suits
Instead of jeans and Timberland boots
Rocking the wrap, instead of the weave
Thinking that in just one look, she can tell my story

Don't let this polish fool you;
I come from the projects
And though I enjoy nice things,
They won't run me into debt

So her insecurity rises to the top;
She's anticipating for yet another reason to hate
Looking for flaws, anything about me
That can be considered fake

I keep to myself,
Avoiding the pettiness of women
No, I don't have the scoop on anyone,
And I don't get involved in competitions

So while she goes to extreme lengths to get men to look her way,
Fishing for enough compliments to boost her self-esteem today
By hugging, kissing, throwing pencils on the floor,
Bending over and silently fuming from all the attention at
    my door

I'm proud of the fact
That I'm secure on the inside
Knowing that I haven't sacrificed my morals for attention;
Thus, I have nothing to hide

I don't flirt, make promises
Or draw attention to my shape
I don't have to switch when I walk
Or use words as bait

Yet my classiness keeps them coming,
As I entice with my overall presence and knowledge
She never ceases to amaze me,
But I'd be more than happy to share some of my polish

Of course, your former friends are surprised when you no longer plunge into the flood of wild and destructive things they do. So they slander you.—1st Peter 4:4 NLT

Face Value

Her eyes told me everything I needed to know
I called her my biggest cheerleader,
But later found her to be a foe

I went along with it,
Pretending we were girls
But I took mental notes of her lies,
For God had warned me to be careful
The deceit was looming in her eyes

I poured my heart out to him
Told myself that he hung in there because he cared
But the truth lay in the emptiness in his eyes
And arose when he assumed I'd share

You see, looks can be deceiving
But eyes are the mirrors of the soul
So people can *pretend* to have the biggest hearts
But their spirits may say they're cold

Many times I tried to ignore the one physical attribute
That never seems to lie
But instead I always used it
To aid me with the strength I needed to say my goodbyes

I've learned that people will pat you on the shoulder with one hand
And with the other stab you from behind
And because we try to be so optimistic,
We pay no attention to the signs

Now there's no use in being paranoid,
But you must come to terms with those who are waiting for your demise
You can tell me you love me all day,
But let me look into your eyes

But if thine eye be evil, thy whole body shall be full of darkness.
—Matthew 6:23

Invasion

I allowed your presence to fill my space,
But I made sure I kept you at arm's length
Brushed off your advances
And changed the subject
When the status of our relationship was mentioned

I couldn't show or tell you
How I really felt
After all, I didn't want to be
Just another notch under your belt

I had to say things, do things
To make you believe I was cold
And no matter what hand you played,
I was determined not to fold

So I stepped on your patience,
Allowed you to finally walk away
I just couldn't risk my heart and pride
By asking if you'd stay

Yes, I lash out when I'm scared
Yet, you braced yourself for the verbal assault
It's hard for me to look in the mirror,
But your intrusion while I'm healing can't *entirely* be my fault

I turned my head
Convinced myself that I wasn't ready to love
I had too many scars
And fear was wearing me like a glove

I look good on paper and from a distance
My pretense of happiness could throw you for a curve
But please find someone that's already whole
Someone who's not scared to reciprocate the love you deserve

I can mess up your life
While carrying this baggage of pain
You've invaded my space
And now my tongue cannot be tamed

Everything was fine,
Until you thought we could be more
And though I'm in the healing process,
My wounds are still sore

This is where we part. I'm sorry.

That was the most difficult poem I have ever had to write (as of today!). To say that it was a struggle would be an understatement! I won't go into too much detail because the wound that inspired it is still fresh. At any rate, I was at a place where I had to ask myself how many relationships I destroyed because of my own fear. I don't think I have enough fingers and toes to count all of the people that I coerced to walk away from me!

What I have been told (and Lord knows I'm not there yet!) is that you have to open up your heart and be able to accept the fact that every relationship is not meant to last forever. Life is about taking risks and one of those risks is letting other people in. It's impossible to live in this world alone. Mummies are usually covered from head to toe; hence, you are not able to see their eyes. If my eyes are covered in my own mummy-like state, then I am not able to see clearly. That's what fear does. It limits your vision. (Somebody needs to preach that!) In my haste to shield myself from people, I wasn't—or haven't been—happy. A part of me wants to trust, but another part of me doesn't think it's worth it.

Wait Your Turn

I'm a janitor. People don't speak to me
They barely glance my way
I'm overlooked, cast to the side
These people don't value or listen to anything I have to say

I'm a teacher
I take pride in what I do
In my own way, I'm giving back to the community
Yet, I know what you mean; I'm overlooked, too

In your life, you may feel unappreciated
Underutilized, waiting for your turn
Wishing that you could maximize your potential
And actually use the skills you've learned

You've sacrificed years of your time
When they never stopped to say thank you
And try as you may to overachieve
You yearn for something new

You may even feel invisible,
Wanting to jump up and say, "I'm right here!"
You don't want to waste your life away
Not achieving your goals is what you fear

Yet you just wait your turn
Your gift will make room
For you to fulfill your wildest dreams
There *is* sunshine behind this gloom

Hold on; wait your turn
This is all preparation
And while they try to hinder your progress,
Continue to get your education

The experience is sure to follow
God is getting ready to open up some doors
And though they won't give you a chance to prove yourself,
I speak into your life that you will never be poor

You're young, educated and driven
You've learned to put Him first
And whether you're a janitor or an usher,
How you're treated does not determine your worth

So whatever your job or career may be,
Don't get bitter; tell God your concerns
And in the meantime, keep your boss and co-workers lifted
 up in prayer
He's an on time God; you just wait your turn

No one from the east or the west or from the desert can exalt a man. But it is God who judges: He brings one down and he exalts another.—Psalms 75:6

PART VI

I Love Me Some Him

While He Slept

I watched you sleep
Wondered about the years that lay before us
I thought about our commitment to God just a few hours ago
My vows to obey, honor, love and trust

I wondered if the curse of infidelity
Had been broken in my blood
Asked myself if I really believed
In unconditional love

I wondered how long it would be
Before we both would begin to change
Could I remain faithful through my pain?
Would you still love me if my body changed?

How long before you start putting in late hours at work?
How will I be able to deal with the Jezebels at church?
Will I have the strength and level of trust in you
To love you through my hurt?

How would we react in the event
That we're unable to conceive and birth children?
Will I have to eavesdrop on your conversations
To see how we're doing?

How much would I have to fight to keep your attention?
When speaking of your greatest achievements,
My name will you mention?
Have you picked the best fruit
Or are you still reaching?

I'm afraid of what the future holds for us
My greatest fear is that you will do something
To cause me to lose trust

As we compromise and make decisions together,
Fulfill our dreams and strive to make our lives better,
Will you need to see if you still "got it," justifying your need to flirt
Did we both really mean for better or for worse?
Will you continue to clean up after yourself?
Will you run to the arms or ears of someone else?

Will you still think I'm beautiful in my rollers and scarf?
Will I be capable of loving you with my whole heart?
God forbid that one of us should fall terminally ill
Would either of us be able to control our flesh
As we wait for Him to heal?

Would you ever hit me?
If it gets rough, will you leave?
If you had to choose between your family and friends,
Would you still choose me?

I'm scared of what we started
These are the questions I've been so afraid to ask
How do I voice my vulnerability?
How do we make our love last?

I Admire You

I admire you, strong Black man
Surviving this game called life,
Giving it all that you can

Your confidence is intriguing
Your intellect is deep
I tried to stroll past you,
But your walk compelled me to speak

You rise up every morning,
Eager to get to work
And with just as much timeliness,
You rush to get to church

Underpaid, ridiculed
The last to get hired
Knew that the color of your skin
Almost guaranteed that you'd be the first one fired

You bounced back, never one to settle
For oppression from The Man
Played the corporate game with the secret members of the
    Ku Klux Klan
Yes, I admire you, strong Black man

Learning from your father's mistakes,
Content with your children and one wife
Putting in crazy overtime
And so willing to sacrifice

Excelled in college, took care of the woman
Who gave birth to you
Gave your life to Christ at a young age
I can't help it, Brother—I admire you

Giving back to the community
Because you've acquired so much
Confident, not arrogant,
Allowing admirers to look but not touch

Putting books in the drug dealers' hands
Promoting Black history 365
Letting them know you understand
But giving them an alternative to getting high

Dealing with your pain
Motivated in spite of it all
Brushing off the negativity
When they anticipated your fall

Cautious around the cops,
Yet not a punk by any means
Mindful that anywhere you go
Could become a potential crime scene

From a sista to a brother,
Do what you gotta do
I just had to stop and say,
"I admire you."

It's no secret that African-Americans or Black people—particularly men—are more likely to be portrayed by the media and its constituents as a group of animalistic, worthless, flashy, jail-bound, illiterate individuals. It seems as if the only time something positive is said about Black people is if they manage to "make it" in sports or the music industry. There are actually some credible, noteworthy African-American men, who may not produce an income of six figures or more, are not beyond average in any sport, and will never sing beyond the walls of their shower. However, they are still wonderful men.

I want to take the time to celebrate these Black men wherever they are, these men who provide for their children and try their best not to let hindrances deter them from making something of themselves. I tip my hat to you.

I know myself what it's like being a young Black woman, striving to prove myself at work where everyone seems to be involved in petty competition, from brown- nosing upper management to comparing shades of skin color. I can't fathom the determined mindset a Black man needs to circumnavigate notorious police officers, store clerks, loan officers and other individuals who label and assume so much about minorities in general. I know what it does to me when I experience these things, but I can't even begin to imagine what my male counterparts are feeling during these offenses.

Yes, I can male-bash with the best of them, but with all my heart and soul, I know that ALL MEN ARE NOT DOGS. So for those men out there who handle your business no matter what obstacles are set against you, I give you a standing ovation. I clap my hands and say, "I admire you."

"Many a man proclaims his own loving-kindness and goodness, but a faithful man who can find?"—Proverbs 20:6

Naked and Not Ashamed

You loved me when I couldn't love myself
Even waited on me when I ran to the arms of someone else
Forgave me repeatedly when I know I did you wrong
Made me feel special when I felt I didn't belong

Provided for me as I exhausted my every resource
Was patient with me when my happiness was forced
Lulled me with soothing words as I fought to get some sleep
Proved that you'd be there no matter what, showing me love unconditionally

Renewed my strength,
Replenished the thirst down in my soul
Softened my heart,
When I felt I had grown too cold

Of all the traits, your forgiveness and long suffering stand out most of all
There were so many times that I thought I'd surely fall
But your love sustained me, kept me from taking my own life
It kept me in the boxing ring—lost a round, but determined to win the fight

I'm hurting, but I don't have the strength to cry
So tired of living, but too afraid to die
I fight to believe every word you've said
Searched for solace when all I really saw was red
I know one day
You're going to make me whole
Naturally I have everything,
But what I need is a healing for my soul

I trust you even though I can't see you

I'm in love with you, and I long to feel your touch
I went out on a limb with this, determined to finally trust
You created me, knew that one day I'd go from victim to victor
Opened up windows when people tried so desperately to close doors

Saw past my issues,
Called me from the womb
You gave me a reason to hold my head up
And the strength to leave my bedroom

Where would I be if you had not taken the time
To free me of the insecurities that once plagued my mind?

I was hurting so much on the inside
I ended up regretting each time I called someone friend
But trouble don't last always
And what I've endured will be worth it in the end

My heart is aching;
Give me the strength to do what I gotta do
Today, I've decided to turn my baggage
Over to you

∽

I tried to give the poem you just read, "Naked and Not Ashamed," the feeling of a relationship between a man and a woman (like in "He Wins") to show how similar it is to salvation. It's about a relationship between you and God. So many people tell me that they are Christians, but being saved requires more than being baptized and saying you believe in God. You know by now that even the devil believes in God (James 2:19). Furthermore, some of the cruelest people have some sort of church or religious affiliation.

In a relationship, you have to start from square one. During this time, you're getting to know each other's, likes and dislikes, etc., and then the relationship is supposed to grow. It is the same way with God. You can't profess salvation and never spend quality time with Him or acknowledge His eminent existence, other than when you need something. Like any relationship, salvation is a never ending process.

In most cases, when you meet someone new, you want your closest friends to know that he or she may be "The One." You spend long hours on the phone or in person and try to do what you can to please that person. It is the same way with God! The main idea here is communication.

A healthy relationship is not off balance. So, your relationship with God should not be "gimme, gimme, gimme" or even the type of relationship where you do all the talking. I've heard preachers often say that God is a gentleman who will not force himself upon you. He is waiting on you to stop running and to stop making excuses for not building a substantial relationship with Him.

If you don't believe He's real, have trust issues, or are not quite sure which religion—if any— you wish to embrace, you have to ask Him for guidance. Sometimes I feel like I'm talking to air, but the Bible lets us know in Hebrews 11:1 that *"Faith is being sure of what we hope for and certain of what we do not see."* When I sat down in this chair to write to you, I believed the chair would hold me up. I didn't test it first. There was no special investigation or research team involved. You have to believe and trust Him. What have you got to lose? You've tried enough new people and ideas; now try Jesus!

"Naked and Not Ashamed" exposes the hurt and doubt I experienced in my walk with God. Trust is an issue that does not sit well with me. Oftentimes, I worry. I worry that I will never heal from all my internal scars. I worry that I will wind up living paycheck to paycheck. I worry that I won't be able to help my family the way I want to, and yes, I even worry whether Mr. Right will ever find me in these tangled bushes I seem to be determined to hide within. After nearly six years of confessing His sovereignty and professing salvation, I still sometimes wonder if I can hold on.

Think about what you want in a relationship partner (emotionally and spiritually, not physically right now!) and see if you're giving those same character traits to God. Can He trust you to carry out His perfect and divine will? No, you're not perfect, but can—and will you—add souls to the kingdom? If you're anything like me, you have your work cut out for you.

Professing salvation and walking in the steps that God has ordered for you is definitely expensive, but it's worth it. I can't imagine where I'd be if I had not fought to build a relationship with God. True salvation requires work. If you're really in love with someone, you don't want to do something that causes that person pain. It is the same way with God. If you're really in love with Him, keep His commandments and follow His precepts. He is long suffering and forgiving. Most of all, He loves you.

I believe the reason why He chose me is because I have always been real with Him. After 'performing' all day in front of my co-workers or people at church, I don't have the energy to be anything else with God. By performing, I mean smiling and making jokes as if everything is all right, when I really want to break down, or sometimes tell some people completely off! Since He created me and knows my innermost thoughts, I can't lie or minimize how I truly feel about certain people or things. There have been some nights when I laid my head on my pillow, determined to backslide (reject God) the very next morning, but because He knew my heart and that I really loved Him, He kept me. He encouraged my spirit and gave me the strength to take it one day a time. How can you *not* love Him?

PART VII

Sista to Sista

I performed the next poem at a talent show. Surprisingly, nearly everyone gave me a standing ovation. It amazed me that so many people could identify with what I was feeling. I have encountered so many people who didn't expect me to go anywhere or be anything. Nevertheless, I not only learned as the song says, *how to live holy,* but I am learning how to be quiet as my gift has made room for me.

In those instances, in not only my work environment, but the church environment as well, I identify closely with King David. He was anointed to be king at a young age, yet he was not appointed until several years later. Nevertheless, David didn't walk around telling people that God had chosen him years earlier to be king over Israel. He remained humble.

Ever since I obtained my first job over a decade ago, I have worked with women who were several years older than I. At the time I didn't know it, but God was preparing me for my calling. I am young in age, but my mindset speaks volumes above the average young adult. So in the natural sense, I have had to hold my head up and be friendless amongst women who were intimidated by my education and how I carried myself. Spiritually, I had to force myself not to get frustrated around people that were stagnant, yet seasoned.

One thing I have learned in the church is that you can be seasoned in age, yet a baby in the spirit. Allow me to translate that for you: Have you ever met someone—say, fifty or sixty years old—who has the audacity to throw temper tantrums or other childish acts as if they're still in grade school? And I'm not talking about people with diagnosed mental illnesses; there are some grown folks out here that will surprise you. You'll end up feeling like you're stuck in a time warp from junior high! I'm here to tell you as a young adult who loves to sit up under women of wisdom, that being or working with someone who doesn't act their age is extremely frustrating.

You should never treat people as if they're merely flies on the wall. Not just because it's mean, but because God always favors underdogs. Who are the underdogs? They are the people you least expect to be anything more than what they are right now or go any further than where they are today. I have been a server, housekeeper, etc. Yet, there is a great anointing over my life. I almost feel sorry for the people who brush me off as if I'm nobody. Then I come to the realization that even in their careless behavior, they are blessing me. My experiences have taught me humility. I've met a lot of individuals that some would consider lowly, but who have an abundance of wisdom inside them.

I once heard a Bishop say, "Who I am and what I do are two totally different things." You don't know who that lady really is standing at the bus stop with four or five kids. She can be the next whoever or the very person you need to get where you need to go. It is never safe to assume that we don't or won't need anybody. My father loves to say, "Sheree, you are not in a world all by yourself."

In the Bible, I'm sure that Joseph's brothers didn't think they'd be seeing him again after what they did either. Yet, he turned out to be the very person they needed in order to avoid starvation and death. You may think I'm just a nobody now, but you don't have any idea where I'm headed!

She Expects Me to Fail

Keeping me out of the loop
Hoping that I'll feel left out
You've been wondering why all the hype
My name brings about

Standing in the shadows
Wishing that I would leave
Smiling in my face—such a disgrace, because I see you
Now, do you see me?

You've been hating on me
To make yourself look good
You think you know me,
Yet my intentions are always misunderstood

Can't figure me out,
Trying to be my friend
I'm cordial,
But you know my guards won't let you in

Watching me,
Constantly tallying up my wrongs
In any attempt
To make me feel like *I* don't belong

Questioning my walk with God,
Convinced that I'm going to hell
What a shame that a *sista*
Is expecting me to fail

Got the 411 on my clothes, my shoes
Talking to people in my circle
In order to get some clues
I just don't know why I'm so important to you

Analyzing me, you think you know
But there's so much more to me than what you see with these here clothes
Nevertheless, in order for me to get here,
I had to take some blows

Still, a compliment from me becomes an ulterior motive
A smile is deemed unreal
You read more into everything I do
In order to assume what I must feel

You're jealous, envious
My success is appalled
It's sad that you can't wait
For me to fall

Wishing I would lose the house, the car,
And God's latter rain
When you should be praying for me,
You're too busy tossing around my name

Putting me down
To make yourself feel better
It's about time
We sistas get it together

I see right through you,
But I'm determined to keep it cool
I'm praying, but know that
When you dig one hole, you better dig two

You're becoming bitter,
Can't wait for my demise
You may think I'm just a secretary,
But you're in for a surprise

There is a wide-open door for a great work here, although many oppose me.—1st Corinthians 16:9 NLT

What's Due

Why can't we as sisters give each other props when they're due?
To compliment someone doesn't take anything away from you
To tell someone they're rockin' that blouse or that skirt
Shouldn't come across as forced, and it definitely shouldn't hurt

I can give you props
Because I can be fly, too
Don't hate on a sista;
Give her what's due!

Why do you have to stare me down?
How is it that you have the audacity
To turn your nose up whenever I'm around?

You don't like your hair?
That can be fixed; buy a weave!
Just because I keep my hair fresh
Shouldn't give you more of a reason to hate on me!

Sista to sista,
Learn how to give props when they're due
Let me walk it out
With my Versace glasses, purse and shoes

It's no problem for me to say I like *your* clothes
When you upgrade yourself,
You have the right to act like you know!
I know you've been overly concerned about your weight
But am I supposed to feel bad
About being a size 8?

They have garments to enhance or minimize
In order for us women to feel and look
As if we're holding the grand prize

You're looking for a flaw,
Something that may be off by a shade
Then you purse your lips
Because my clothes are custom made

Stop being insecure and step up your game
It's sad that most of my enemies don't even know my name!
But they know what I'm thinking: "I'm all that."
Please believe it, sista—now where *your* confidence at?

After years of holding my head down
Feeling as if I was the ugly duckling, the inevitable black sheep
I've added some pep to my step
Now please, don't hate on me

Yet, after all was said and done
It wasn't even about me and how I keep myself "fenced"
It was about your own insecurity
And lack of confidence

"I am for peace, but when I speak, they are for war."—Psalms 120:7

Power of the Body

Work it girl,
Show 'em what you're working with!
But then why are you mad
Because he just wanna hit?

Your skirt could be mistaken for a handkerchief
And can you breathe in those pants?
You're barely dressed,
Yet you think y'all just gonna sit and hold hands?

Tonight? Oh, no boo!
Your breasts are falling out of your shirt
If you're not for sale, take your sign down
Show a man what you're worth!

Women, young and old,
There's power in our curves
But we can't let our bodies make decisions for our spirit
Because a man's power lies in his words

No, you can't totally hide the hourglass
You can't cover up the shape
But if you love and respect yourself
You won't sacrifice your reputation with the decisions you make

Leave some mystery
And please don't let it all hang out
You *say* you're not a whore,
But he's not looking at your mouth

When you have power over something,
You shouldn't just give it away
So if a man wants to leave,
Don't forfeit your power in order to make him stay

Lure him with the aura of your presence
You want to stand out, then don't be like everybody else
You don't even have to say anything
Your classiness will speak for itself!

Ladies, we have the power to make men stride into walls
Stumble, have accidents, take the risk of getting caught
All for a peek at the power,
Not to mention our walk

Don't compare yourself to other women
God has given you everything that you need
Sista, there's power inside each of us
Use *that* to succeed.

Ladies, ladies, ladies, what are we wearing these days? When I was in my teens, I got a kick out of the reaction I received from men as I flaunted some of my most revealing attire. There were basically no men in my life, so I thrived for male attention, whether it was positive or negative. I further knew I had it going on when the women around me stared and complimented me. I was starving for attention and I loved it. That was a phase I went through. I later realized how beautiful I am and the different type of men I attracted when I stopped showing my ribcage and thighs!

It's a shame that our young girls are no longer leaving anything to the imagination. And the men can be just as bad (If *I* can fit your shirt, then we have a problem, but that's an entirely different book!) I participated in a class promoting self-esteem and I informed the teens and pre-teens that if they really loved and respected themselves, they wouldn't feel the need to expose their bodies for the world to see. I empathize with them because I know what it's like to want men to want you, yearning to be desired and noticed, especially when there is no father in the home. However, I can now throw on a T-shirt and jeans on any given day and not feel unattractive because I'm secure in myself. Confidence is what it's all about.

What's even worse is when I see women old enough to be my mother wearing next to nothing. I feel so sorry for them for still feeling the need to show off their bodies. I don't know if it has to do with them having a midlife crisis or if they are excited about the weight they may've recently lost. Nevertheless, there should come a time in your life where you look in the mirror and realize you're grown. In 1st Corinthians 13:11, it says, *"When I was a child, I talked like a child; I thought like a child, I reasoned like a child. When I became a man (or woman), I put childish ways behind me."*

I heard this Bishop say that women are always complaining that men only want them for their bodies. He said that men are complaining about women only wanting them for their money. The preacher surmised that we attract certain people because of what we display. He said that if you want somebody to love you for your mind, then you need to show your mind. Henceforth, whenever I go out with a member of the opposite sex, I put forth a greater effort to cover as much as possible, without appearing to be a nun, of course!

I want to be most remembered for who I am on the inside and not simply for what I look like on the outside. Anybody can 'buy' a great body these days, but who are you behind the silicone, implants, weave and numerous surgeries? Your inner substance is what's going to make relationships last, whereas your pulchritude is only skin deep. Someone once told me that the most important thing in the cemetery is the dash between the year a person is born and the year they depart this life. The dash represents who the person was and what they did while they were here. It has nothing to do with the way they looked on the outside.

Have you ever met somebody that was F-I-N-E, only to find out that the person was U-G-L-Y on the inside? I don't want to be that way (anymore!), so that's why I've been focusing on healing these wounds, ridding myself of the baggage that has been weighing me down and hindering me from developing meaningful relationships. It is also the reason why I stopped shopping so much. I want to concentrate on healing what's on the inside, because that's what counts the most.

I heard someone say that the more bling you have, the lower your self-esteem. That statement is so true because I used to think I had to have the matching purse, shoes, sunglasses, and jewelry to go along with every outfit, or else I wasn't on point. Don't get me wrong. I still think appearance and perception are important, but I don't take it to the extreme where I'm running up credit cards and causing my bank account to suffer.

There is more to me than what meets the eye. I'm still discovering things about myself; that's why I get offended when men pursue me with the intent to sleep with me and then walk away. After all I've been through, I will not be used.

Ammunition

You roll your eyes
When I enter the room
And any mention of my success
Leaves you fumed

You're mocking the fact that I'm single,
But know that it's because I can
Allowing God to heal my hurt
Is a concept you'd never understand

Every time you turn around,
Someone is mentioning my name
And your lackluster attempt at conversation
Is really quite a shame

So instead of wondering what I've done
To cause you to turn up your nose
I'll let you talk about me, lie on me
And attempt to find flaws with my clothes

I now use your energy as ammunition,
A fuel if you will
And while you continue to play games,
I'm determined to keep it real

I stopped trying to figure out
What I did to you
Instead I use success as the best revenge,
And do what I gotta do

I like to think I'm open,
Always willing to talk things out
But until you're ready to tell me what's up,
Then we really don't have anything to talk about

Because of your insecurities,
You feel as if we're in competition
And while your mind is on soap operas,
My mind is on tuition

Looking for ways to better myself
Not settling for the measure of my worth through the eyes of someone else
Who has the best hairstyle?
Who's the best dressed?
How much do I think your outfit cost?
Trust me when I say I couldn't care less

Nevertheless, I need people like you in my life
To give me a reason to dust off and move on
Yes, it's because of you
That I'm compelled to wake up at the break of dawn

Working out, keeping my shape
Knowing when to be punctual
And when to be fashionably late
Not looking for someone representing the guise of a soul mate

While I wait on God to bless me with him,
You decide to poke fun
Telling me how silly I am
To wait for The One

I can feel your dislike
And I know my presence gets under your skin
I hate to be the one to break it to you,
But I didn't come here to make friends

I will no longer minimize myself
To make you feel good
And now I wash my hands,
Knowing that I did every thing I could

I pushed you into the job market,
Encouraged you to fulfill your wildest dreams
Gave you tips on the stock market
And how to keep your credit clean

Prayed and fasted with you
And we even cried together
As I worked my way up,
I tried to motivate you to do better

No matter how much I tried to understand you,
Giving you props when they were due
It still wasn't good enough,
But thanks for the fuel

Ouch, right? Yes, but by now you know that I have had some issues building sister-to-sister relationships. As you may have already surmised, I'm not exactly a people person. For the majority of my life, I have been a loner and now that I'm putting forth an effort to spread my wings, I'm faced with a ton of challenges. I said this before, but my greatest problem is getting people to understand me. I am extremely sarcastic and have a dry sense of humor; however, I have found that once people spend a reasonable amount of time around me, they seem to understand me even less!

I once had this "heated fellowship" with an individual. What I liked most about this person was that we could talk about literally anything for hours. I'm not a shallow person by any means, so I love a good, stimulating conversation. I allowed myself to get comfortable in our friendship and felt that if we ever had a problem, we would be able to simply talk it over. Big mistake!

One day, this person practically read me my rights over the phone, and all I could do was cry and hold my head down. Not because they were right or I felt guilty, but because I had done everything I could to be upfront and real. I had no idea this person had felt the depth of resentment they had for me. I prayed to God over and over, constantly wondering what I did to cause this person to dislike me as much as they did. The exchange had left me feeling as if I really didn't know this person at all, especially since I was thinking we had a decent friendship and an overall understanding of one another.

Nevertheless, instead of me shutting down the way I would have several months before, I used all of my negative experiences with building new relationships with men and women as fuel to write "Ammunition." It was a learning experience, and I felt grateful that I took a chance on developing a relationship with a new person after all. Even though taking the risk backfired, I would definitely do it over again.

I have heard that I am a really good listener, which is the reason why I have a lot of heart-to-heart talks with different people. I've also found that the things they previously assumed about me tend to be incredibly far from the truth. I can admit that I have some . . . ways . . . but I know I'm a good person and I won't spend the rest of my life trying to prove that to people (especially women) who are wrestling with their own insecurities and as a result, try to force *me* to pay the consequences.

It has become very frustrating for me as I have tried to be more friendly and receptive to people in general, only to find out that yet another person has this huge misconception of me and my motives for doing things the way I do them. I have had the same four friends for well over a decade. I am content with these people, because they know enough about me to not be overly sensitive around me. I don't just say things without caring for someone else's feelings, but if you specifically ask for my opinion (and sometimes even if you don't) I will tell you exactly how I feel. God has been working with me in order for me to say certain things in a gentler way, due to the fact that He has called us to draw people with loving kindness (Jeremiah 31:3).

"Ammunition" was written describing a series of my experiences while trying to cultivate relationships with people. I have seriously been burned by women, and even some men who may have thought they could tell my story or assume certain things about me. However, Laquania Graham cannot be figured out that easily. If you were to ask a variety of people—at church, work, school or wherever—what they think about me, there would definitely be a mixed response. You would NEVER get the same answer. I've heard that I can be very sweet, downright mean and everything in between, so you can't just label me and put me in a box for storage.

"Ammunition" is my favorite poem because I have been so worried and hurt while spending many hours explaining myself, apologizing and trying to understand what I may have said or done to make certain people come to so many false conclusions about me. For example, have you ever said 'x' and someone tried to read deeper into x, only to conclude 'y'? This is beyond frustrating because I don't operate with a hidden agenda. Either I am a member of your fan club or praise section, or I don't bother with you at all.

A good number of people who know me pretty well describe me as being mostly "all bark and no bite." I hate to admit it, but that statement is true. However, when I do bite, you may end up talking about it for years! I feel like I have to protect myself from people hurting me. I oftentimes find myself resenting people who are so open to everybody because I feel like they set themselves up to be hurt. At the same time, I'm jealous because they're not carrying the load I am. They find the strength to love again in spite of what they've been through, and I can't manage to let go!

What I have continuously found throughout my many ordeals is that there has to be a happy medium. You cannot be so caught up in your world of seclusion (of which I am so guilty) that you don't enjoy life for what it is worth. Furthermore, you cannot function and establish a good working relationship with anybody while going through life in a nonchalant manner.

Sometime during late 2006 and early 2007, I had been on this quest to become friendlier and participate in recreational activities outside of my best friend of twelve years and my immediate family. During this time there were two women in my life who I thought exhibited a reasonable degree of philosophical intelligence, or simply put, they were cool. So I decided to take our conversation and venue to the next level. Shortly after initiating some quality time to get to know these women, I concluded that they weren't the type of people I wanted to hang out with outside of our regular setting. Both of them had severely hurt my feelings in different ways, and I instantly became angry with myself for stepping outside of the box.

True to form, my best friend gave me some excellent advice. She told me not to look at every new person as being a potential best friend. Some people are great for shopping, some are great for just hanging out on the weekends, and some are extraordinary conversationalists. What she was trying to get me to realize is that I should accept the person for the place they represent in my life. So, if Ms. Great Shopping Partner knows how to help you put accessories and clothes together but can't hold a decent conversation, don't try to make her into something she is not. Accept her for who she is. You will seldom find a friend or associate that encompasses all of the qualities you like, but accept and respect that individual for what they contribute to your life.

God has been chastising me in the area of unconditional love. I'm not exempt from His reprimands because of anything that I have done in any way. Whenever I come across that scripture I mentioned earlier regarding only loving those that love you (Matthew 5:46-47), I instantly feel guilty and am faced with the one area which I feel I am lacking in the most, and that is serving the Lord with unconditional love for others.

I came across a quote by G. K. Chesterton that I absolutely loved. It said, "The Bible tells us to love our neighbors, and also to love our enemies, probably because they are generally the same people." That particular quote put me in inner turmoil because I had to realize that in my haste to only like people who like me, I was assuming that I knew all of my foes. A lot of people pretend to be for you when in all actuality they are against you. They would like for you to believe that they are indeed your friend. In such cases, I nod my head and go through the motions. It's not that I'm being phony; it's just that I might get a certain vibe from an individual, even though they haven't come right out and admitted that they don't particularly care for me. I just get this feeling...

Whatever the underlying motive or intent, I am learning to use the negative energy—or feeling— I get from my haters as fuel. Fuel for me to do whatever it takes to fulfill my destiny. For instance, let me find out that I have an enemy or hater at a party or social gathering. I pull out all the stops, from the outfit to the nails! I want the person to know that no matter what they may think or feel about me, they cannot stop me from being happy and feeling good about myself.

I challenge you to employ the same philosophy. There may be people in your life who are full of negative energy and may have called you everything but a child of God, but know that success is the best revenge, not only in the natural or material sense (because anybody can do that), but in your state of mind. Let God heal you and use you for His glory. People will begin to look at you and wonder what it is that makes you smile for no reason, walk with your head up and look like everything is perfect in your life when it really is a mess. Faith in God does that for you. It causes you to believe Him even when your situation doesn't make sense. Amen, church?

I sometimes visit Pastor R.A. Vernon at The Word Church in Cleveland, Ohio. He said something that made me jump out of my seat: "If you didn't like me before, you're about to get madder and madder." I say, "For everyone that may have written me off, you ain't seen nothin' yet."

Afterword

Thank you for spending so much time with me on my journey of going even deeper. I pray that these poems and brief narratives have been therapeutic for you. I pray that God fulfills your desire to be whole and that you accept His will. His will may cause you to sever some relationships. You may even have to be alone for some time while He places you under construction, but there is a healing for your soul.

When you awoke this morning, you didn't take one huge deep breath that was supposed to last the entire day. No, you are constantly breathing. Life is full of constants and guarantees. You will constantly have to be your own cheerleader if you want to get anywhere in life. You will constantly have to make sacrifices for your loved ones. It's a guarantee that you will not always be happy. It is a guarantee that life will not always go your way, no matter how much money or power you have. But if I could give you three things (that I hope you have already construed by now), they would be:

Don't settle
Don't compromise
Love yourself

You have to maximize your potential, and be careful to not sacrifice your happiness for luxury. You have one life to live, one chance to pull it all off. Now what are you going to do with it?

Do you believe that I am able to do this? They said unto him, Yes, Lord.—Matthew 9:28

Acknowledgements

I promise this will be a lot shorter than last time!

God, you are indeed my everything. Thank you for breaking the mold when you brought me into this world. Thank you for being:

- My friend when I needed someone to talk to
- My comforter and shield as I took the blows of life
- My encourager when people looked down on me and my work
- My provider when all I had was 'two fish and five loaves of bread'
- My strength when I felt like throwing in the towel
- My rock when the closest people to me seemed uncertain
- My healer when I didn't have the strength to stand up

Thank you for the whispers on my pillow, and the dreams, visions and vials of tears you collected from me. I know that I am precious in your sight and I was not only called, but chosen. I certainly would not be where I am today if you hadn't taken the time to shape and mold me. I love you and trust that you'll make everything all right. Thank you for using me, even in my brokenness.

Mom, thank you for being my biggest fan, no matter what I set my mind to do. You are the epitome of unconditional love. God couldn't have blessed me with a better mother. Dad, I am grateful to you for pushing me and instilling so many quotes and pearls of wisdom inside me. Thank you for constantly reminding me how proud I have made you. Coming from you, that means a lot!

To my sisters and brothers, I love you. Dr. Pam, don't give up. I need you to treat my kids when I decide to have some!

To Jermaine, thank you for pushing me into the spotlight. I am thankful for our relationship and I can't wait 'til you shine! God has called you for such a time as this, and I know it's only a matter of time before you walk into those doors that have been waiting on you. Now, let's work on Part 3!

To my nieces and nephews across the globe, mad love. I'm doing my part to pave the way for you. I am living proof that there is nothing you can't do.

To Talin (my bff!), Veronica (my bcf!), Addarryll, Sabrina, Antoine, The Fam and Joseph, thank you for allowing me to vent as I struggled to let my guard down. Your patience through my healing process is a story all in itself!

A special thank you is granted to the illustrious Yvonne Pointer who pushed me into the limelight. What a blessing it is to meet someone who doesn't mind sharing her space and resources. Thank you for showing me by example that there is enough money out here for all of us!

Positive Plus, thank you all for waiting on me. You waited for me to heal and didn't push me when I clammed up and ran away. Save my tissue box because I'm about to be free!

Mother Moore, thank you for not letting me give up. You wouldn't even let me cry! I'm so glad God saw fit to allow our paths to cross. I didn't know how much I needed you in my corner, until you showed up. I love you.

Pastor Tiger and Lady Bradley, thank you for your support and encouragement. You sowed into my ministry and made me feel loved when I almost gave up on church people. I am so thankful to God for placing you both in my life.

To Sarah Williams, who I hope I've given enough fuel to pursue each career and personal endeavor: girl, you going places!

Thanks to all of the newspapers and book clubs, and talk shows both on TV and radio, especially Ilinda Reese of *Taking Care of Business*, who made me feel so comfortable. It truly takes a special gift to do that.

I am also indebted to so many people who sincerely supported my brother and me. All of the e-mails that hailed words of encouragement, personal testimonies and the phone calls have not gone unnoticed as we pursued our endeavors.

Celeste Terry of the United Black Fund in Cleveland, Ohio, thank you for "getting" my poems. You had a way of making me open up without being offensive or nosy. That takes skill!

To my editor, Leah Whitney, my book would not be as polished as it is without your incredible talent. With all the experience and expertise you possess, it boosted my self-esteem to know that my work spoke volumes to you. Your continuous words of encouragement and praise have convinced me that I am a pretty good writer after all.

Thanks to Monique Goings for doing a *fabulous* job on my cover photo and design. May God reward you for what you've done on my behalf.

To all of my co-workers who continued to push (and push, and push) me to fulfill my dreams and encourage me when I felt like throwing in the towel, thank you. I can't count the number of people that cheered me on when all I could do was shake my head…

And last but not least, to all of the people who contributed so much to the development of this book, whether it came as a result of a negative or a positive experience, thank you. I certainly could not have done this without each and every one of you.

As writer, orator, motivator and mentor, Laquania "Sheree" Graham knows no boundaries. She has appeared on talk shows, in newspapers and has even been featured on the radio as a result of her debut titled, *My Soul on Paper* which was co-authored with her talented younger brother, Jermaine Jackson.

Laquania obtained a Bachelor of Arts degree from Cleveland State University with a concentration in Urban Service Administration. She is currently pursuing a Master's degree in Public Administration.

If you would like to invite the author to your venue for speaking engagements, youth ministry workshops, or would like information on how to purchase additional books, please contact Laquania Graham by email or regular mail:

www.mysoulonpaper.com
or
My Soul on Paper c/o Laquania Graham
PO BOX 35565
Cleveland, Ohio 44135

May God bless and keep you....

Printed in the United States
100046LV00002B/43-63/A